EVERYDAY LIFE IN EARLY AMERICA

THE EVERYDAY LIFE IN AMERICA SERIES

EDITED BY

RICHARD BALKIN

To Judith

CONTENTS

Illustrations follow pages 52 and 116.

INTRODUCTION

There are several points to make at the start. The first is to justify a book such as this. Johan Huizinga has done that in *The Waning of the Middle Ages,* wherein he says,

> The specific forms of the thought of an epoch should not only be studied as they reveal themselves in theological and philosophical speculations, but also as they appear in practical wisdom, and every day life. We may even say that the true character of the spirit of the age is better revealed in its mode of regarding and expressing trivial and commonplace things than in the high manifestations of philosophy and science.

The second point comes as advice from James Deetz's *In Small Things Forgotten.*

> Were we to confront a seventeenth century Anglo-American we would experience a sense of culture shock as profound as if we had encountered a member of any other of the world's exotic cultures. We mistakenly think of Americans in the seventeenth century as ourselves but somehow simpler, "quaint" perhaps, but people with whom we would feel an instant empathy. In fact, [their] world was assembled according to a different set of rules. . . . Recognizing this fundamental difference permits us to consider the people of that time more in their own terms, rather than in those categories we impose on them.

Deetz's advice must be taken with a touch of salt. The past has not, as it might seem, been obliterated from our culture. The folk medicine of early America still survives in isolated areas. Russell Baker recalls in his autobiography, *Growing Up,* that "witch-doctoring" prevailed in the Virginia he knew in the 1920s. A local physician unable to cure a facial rash sent Baker's sister to an old woman known for remedies that dated back doubtless to seventeenth-century America. ("But don't you dare tell anybody I sent you to her," he warned.) When youngsters today learn that "thirty days hath September, April, June, and November," they repeat a verse seventeenth-century American youngsters were reared on. Early immigrants anxiously awaited Candlemas, an English religious festival celebrated on February 2, but not necessarily for its religious significance.

> If Candlemas Day be fair and bright,
> Winter will have another fright;
> But if it be dark with clouds and rain,
> Winter is gone and will not come again.

The day is still awaited by many in America, only under a new name—Groundhog Day.

Although relics from the past do survive, the everyday life of seventeenth-century Americans differed drastically from ours. As Fernand Braudel, like Deetz, reminds us, to comprehend it we must "strip ourselves in imagination of all the surroundings of our own lives." The journey backward, he adds, "is a journey to another planet, another human universe."

1

O STRANGE
NEW WORLD?

WHO CAME AND WHY THEY CAME · WHAT THEY BROUGHT WITH THEM · WHAT THEY FOUND

Who Came and Why They Came

To hear the seventeenth century tell it, only the dregs came this way—"unruly gallants packed thither by their friends to escape ill destines . . . condemned wretches, forfeited by law . . . strumpets and bawds, for the abomination of life spewed out of their country . . . poor gentlemen, broken tradesmen, rakes and libertines, footmen and such others fitter to spoil or ruin a commonwealth than to help to raise and maintain one." The mayor of Bristol told the king that among those who went "some are husbands, some are children and apprentices run away from their parents and masters; . . . and many have been pursued by hue-and-cry for robberies, burglaries or breaking prison, do thereby escape the prosecution of law and justice."

But the mayor and others only sought to reassure the Crown that it lost to America people of no importance. Some did come against their will—criminals given the choice of death or immigration, vagrants, orphaned children, paupers, those judged "lewd and dangerous," and, of course, enchained blacks. But the bulk of emigrants came voluntarily, and more often than not they were the most "vivid people" of England, those with energy and courage enough to make a new start in life. The undernourished poor, sapped physically and psychologically, seldom ventured overseas except under duress. Most of those who emigrated were from what would be called today the middle and lower-middle classes—farmers, shopkeepers, artisans, and, yes, lively, saucy young women in search of husbands. Perhaps there is truth in the remark of a contemporary, that "God sifted an whole nation that He might bring choice grain over into this wilderness."

The character of the emigration created something close to an equal society, unlike anything known then in England or, for that matter, in all of Europe. Old attitudes toward social status remained intact, but in economic terms the distance between the bottom and the top of society was relatively slight. Occasionally, in the early years, gentlemen did cross to America. In Virginia they soon vanished; if they lived through the "seasoning" that killed so many, they sailed home with blistered hands and emaciated bodies, convinced that for all its faults a more benign England offered a better way of life. In New England and the Middle Colonies many stayed and, for the most part, exerted a lasting influence on society and everyday life. Still, the generalization holds that most of the emigrants emerged from England's middle and lower-middle classes.

America through the seventeenth century was chiefly a land of farmers, and the illusion persists that most of those who first arrived knew much about tilling the land. William Bradford, long a governor of Plymouth Plantation, helped to create this illusion. The Pilgrims, he said, "were not acquainted with trade nor traffic . . . but had only been used to a plain country life and the innocent trade of husbandry." But the Pilgrims had for some time lived urban lives in Holland; the majority were artisans of one sort or another. William Brewster, their leader, had been a village postmaster and superintendent of a local manor. John Carver, another governor, had been a printer. Myles Standish was a professional soldier. And Bradford himself had not put his hand to a plow since the age of seventeen. Even those outsiders on the *Mayflower*, "strangers" to the Pilgrims' religious views, were not necessarily farmers. John Alden, of "speak for yourself, John" fame, was a cooper (barrel-maker) by trade. The same nonagrarian background holds for those who went to Massachusetts. They came from agrarian counties, true, but most were craftsmen—weavers, tailors, coopers, brewers, shoemakers, and the like. Out of three hundred heads of households whose trades are known only seventy-five were yeomen or husbandmen, that is, farmers. A sixth of those three hundred came from London. Those who emigrated to Virginia were also urbanites. The speech of early Virginia was "the speech of London."

Historians still lack good data about the backgrounds of the vast majority of early settlers, but, as one scholar remarks cautiously, "it does seem to be the case in most colonies that craftsmen and people from 'urban' backgrounds were disproportionately represented and that many who ended up as farmers in America were not that before." Why then did apparently a minority of English farmers come to America, at least in the beginning? Howard S. Russell, in *A Long, Deep Furrow*, gives an answer.

> Consider what was involved. Each countryman had to sell or lease his land, or if a tenant, abandon his copyhold, renouncing cherished ancestral or acquired rights and privileges. He had then to provide himself with tools and equipment for his new enterprise; and to pay the heavy cost of transporting household goods, and livestock 3,000 miles. He had to provide in advance supplies for the subsistence of his family, servants, and stock, for many months after arrival. To these financial considerations must be added a farmer's inborn conservatism and the uncertainties connected with farming everywhere, any time, but especially in an unknown land and climate.

Now, what propelled people to America? Those who first went to Virginia expected, hoped for, quick wealth; the London Company's propaganda had suggested they would find it there. The desire to worship as they pleased sent many to New England and the Middle Colonies. But there were more general motives for leaving the homeland. Economic pressure prodded hundreds to make the long leap into the dark; a string of bad harvests and several severe winters, coupled with intermittent commercial depressions in the early part of the seventeenth century, had left large parts of the population deprived, to say the least, perhaps even close to starvation. Still others, appalled at the changes the early Stuarts were imposing on England's social, political, and religious life, saw America as a place to retain old customs in a shifting universe. "The world's in a heap of troubles and confusions," one man said, "and while they are in the midst of the changes and amazes, the best way to give them the bag is to go out of the world and leave them."

Contented people do not emigrate as a rule, but neither, necessarily, do discontented people. Those who came were only a fraction of the population of England in the seventeenth century. Private, some might say trivial, reasons often determined the decision to emigrate. A sixteen-year-old boy departed because his father "toke a stick and basted me [when] I went to dansing scoll to larne to dans." The end of a love affair sent some men over the ocean. Greed drew many. A clergyman came because his friends were going and "my dear wife much longed to see me settled there in peace, and so put me to it." Some sent their sons to the wilderness to be tamed, others went solely "for merchandise and gain's sake."

Whatever motives pushed them across the surly ocean, no one came eager to shed his English past. Whether they saw America as the land where failures got a second chance, an oasis where they could worship as they wished, or the place where a vanishing past could be preserved, all set out determined to remain what most of them were—Englishmen.

What They Brought with Them

But what was an Englishman? England in the early seventeenth century was a society "neither stagnant nor uniform," but rather one "experiencing great dynamic change." There was an astonishing diversity to local life. It varied not only regionally but from county to county, even village to village. John Fowles, in *The French Lieutenant's Woman,* speaks about this diversity among the plain people of Victorian England, but his remarks apply equally well to those of the seventeenth century.

> It is difficult to imagine today the enormous differences then separating a lad born in Seven Dials and a carter's daughter from a remote East Devon village. Their coming together was fraught with almost as many obstacles as if he had been an Eskimo and she, a Zulu. They had barely a common language, so often did they not understand what the other had said.

In the seventeenth century the girl may have been reared in a thatched hut, the boy in a stone house with a slate roof. Her father may have been accustomed to the open-field system of farming, tending his strips of land in common with other farmers of the community and herding his cattle on the village green. The lad may have come from a county where farmers worked their own fenced-in plots of land when and as they wished. Both doubtless were Protestants, but she may have been a dissenting Puritan while he relaxed within the Church of England's ritual. To America each brought "a blueprint in their minds for re-creating the culture they had left behind." Any marriage between them seemed, indeed, fraught with obstacles.

Still, they shared much in common. Both knew that all society deferred to the king and then to the nobility, but that the gentry ran the nation. By custom the clergy, university graduates, lawyers, physicians, military officers, and virtually anyone who "can live without manual labor" could sign themselves "gent," but generally land and gentility went together. Gentlemen were not necessarily genteel; they could be as bawdy and vulgar as the lowest in England. But as "the garrisons of good order throughout the realm," they alone outside those in the armed forces had the right to bear arms. They alone served in the House of Commons, and as justices of the peace they were the law of the countryside. If few gentlemen came to America, many of their younger sons, deprived of an inheritance by the rules of primogeniture and entail (by which all land in the family went in bulk to the eldest son), did come, and they brought the traditions of the gentry with them.

Below the gentry stood the yeomen. They owned or leased enough land—a forty-shilling freehold, so called, or approximately fifty acres—which gave them the right to vote, and though they invariably chose gentlemen to fill the more important positions, they occasionally found themselves elected to minor posts. Below the yeomen spread the mass of "laboring poor"—hired laborers, poor husbandmen who rented small plots of land, tailors, shoemakers, masons, and other craftsmen. They comprised 95 percent of England's population and had "neither voice nor authority in the commonwealth" but were "to be ruled and not to rule others." The poor of England lacked all rights. They could be conscripted to work in mines, impressed into the army and navy, jailed for being unemployed. Their wages were fixed low by law and made lower still by a slow but steady inflation. About a quarter of these people often lived on the edge of starvation.

The barriers between classes were not insurmountable. A talented lad could travel up to London, progress from lowly clothier to rich merchant, then return to the country, buy an estate and call himself a gentleman. But the movement up—or down—did not erase differences between classes. A man's dress instantly betrayed his rank. So, too, did his speech. "Your accent is something finer than you purchase in so removed a dwelling," one Shakespearean character accuses another in disguise. A bow, a curtsy, the doffing of a hat kept distinctions alive. Servants were addressed as "thee," equals as "you." A gentleman's coach gave way to a nobleman's. Each class had its own sports; a yeoman played ninepins, a gentleman bowled.

An Englishman's life revolved first around his family—"a little church, and a little commonwealth, . . . a school wherein the first principles and grounds of government and subjection are learned." The male head ruled absolutely in law, relatively in fact, for "of all that are inferiors, the wife comes nearest to parity." English women enjoyed more freedom than those on the Continent. By law they inherited at least part of their husband's estate, no regulations prevented them from marrying the man they wished, and tradition argued that the wife should share in all major decisions. "If the pilot would labor at the pump, and do all himself, it must needs go ill with the ship," went one injunction regarding tyrannical husbands. The strength of the family did not mean that happiness pervaded it. The absconding husband seeking to escape from a shrew was common. Cases of adultery, incest, sodomy, and other "uncleanness and wickedness of life" filled the ecclesiastical courts.

Superstition, coupled with a belief in witchcraft and astrology, flourished, but so, too, did a respect for education. Over nine hundred grammar schools existed in England in 1640, one for virtually every large town and most of the smaller ones; they were free to the poor. If a son seemed slow or little interested in books, the family apprenticed him at puberty or earlier. A bonded servant became part of the family of his master, whose role legally was that of a surrogate father responsible for the apprentice's spiritual, moral, and physical well-being.

An Englishman's life revolved, secondly, around his village or town. A family's concerns seldom extended beyond local horizons. About 70 percent of the nation lived in or close by a country village, another 25 percent in large towns; 5 percent, or between two or three hundred thousand out of a population of perhaps four and a half million, lived in London. These figures for London can be misleading. It has been pointed out that a danger to avoid in talking about the English village on the eve of colonization is to overstate the static quality of life within it. A large transient population constantly moving into London from the countryside, and then after a spell returning home, served as a conduit to the rural world of the latest fashions in clothing, housing, cooking, and a host of other innovations affecting everyday life.

No doubt these imports from the great city influenced village life, but how deeply they penetrated downward from the gentry, who often welcomed them, to the plain people is open to question. It can be argued that traditions dating back to the Middle Ages, from which England had only recently emerged, continued to dominate rural life. The heavy, ornate chest of medieval design into which emigrants packed cherished belongings to take to America gave visible presence of the past's hold over the present. Youngsters were taught the medieval notion that what they did reflected first on the family, then rippled out to affect the entire community. Whether they became craftsmen, merchants, or farmers, they knew from youth that no man was an island, that their lives and actions were inextricably involved with the welfare of the community. Town fathers regulated the products that citizens brought to market —judging the quality, the weight, the justness of the price—and no one questioned their right to do so. (This is not to say that cheating did not prevail; ideals seldom flourish in everyday life.) When someone died in a seventeenth-century English village, no one needed an explication of John Donne's lines, "Do not send to ask for whom the bell tolls. It tolls for thee."

As for government, a point to iterate about everyday life in England as well as early America is made by a modern scholar: "National affairs only dimly influenced people. It was what happened on the local scene that mattered." The historian fascinated by the large story tends often to forget that the average Englishman of the day knew little about national affairs. The royal government rarely intruded on his everyday life. A host of officials did intrude—constables, well-masters, ale-tasters, clerks of the market, hog-ringers, and so forth—but these were local men concerned with local matters. The single familiar royal official on the local scene was the justice of the peace, chosen by and responsible to the Crown but a man from the community. Invariably, he came from the gentry, for "no poor man ought to be in authority," said a gentleman, because he "will so bribe you and extort you that the sweet scent of riches and gain taketh away and confoundeth the true state of justice and equity." The office could be an exasperating burden, but one few gentlemen dared to refuse; it was an honor to receive, a duty to accept, and a training ground for those eager to serve in Parliament.

A justice of the peace carried heavy administrative duties. He fixed wages, licensed alehouses and checked that they observed hours, apprenticed boys to trades, found homes for orphans, saw to the care of the poor and infirm, disciplined the obstreperous, inspected roads and bridges, punished all legal infractions, large and small. He kept, or was supposed to keep, the king's ministers informed on all aspects of local life that might be relevant to the welfare of the nation. The increasing number of impositions upon him from London under the early Stuarts convinced some of the justices they had little to lose in moving to America.

The justice, rarely versed in law, guided himself through a legal jungle by common sense, local customs, and whatever he could pick up from any of many "how-to" books available everywhere. In serious cases he generally let the accused stand free on bail—jails were few and men could not be kept long from their shops or plots of land if families were to survive—until he met with colleagues from other parts of the county in quarter sessions court, which could try all crimes except treason and offenses by servants of the Crown. The English of the day were a litigious people and warmed to a good trial. ("Every

ploughman with us . . . can talk of essoins, vouchers, wither-
mans, and recaptions," said a lawyer in 1602.) They held a low
opinion of the law, calling it a "babblative art"; they knew that
judges could be bribed, that decisions tended to favor gentlemen, and that only the "meaner sort" received physical punishment. They also knew that for all that the legal system worked.
Hearings were open, which helped to minimize flagrant unfair-
ness; juries were only occasionally pressured into outright dis-
honest decisions.

The justice's orders were executed by the constable—often
called petty constable to distinguish him from the sheriff, or
high constable, a county official appointed by the Crown. The
constable was usually a yeoman, born and reared in the village
and well acquainted with its idiosyncracies. He apprehended
thieves, chased vagrants, collected fines, and in general served
as the village police force. He worked closely with the churchwarden, a layman chosen by an exclusive group within the
church that eventually came to be known as the vestry. The
break with Rome had deposited much of the property and
many of the duties of the monasteries in the lap of the local
parish, which, in effect, meant the village, for they were often
one and the same. The churchwarden, collaborating with the
justice of the peace and the constable, supervised the care of
the poor, the infirm, and the aged, and arranged for the rearing
of illegitimate and orphaned children. He also rented church
property and gathered the tithes.

The Anglican church had taken shape under Elizabeth I, who
sought to produce a mild and eclectic Protestantism that would
alleviate tensions within an England that had so recently been
Catholic. It was a state church, its doctrines determined and its
leaders selected by the Crown. It embraced the whole community; indeed, the parish church was a community center, a
meetinghouse, as well as a place of worship. It retained much
from the Roman Catholic past—the episcopal hierarchy, holy
days, vestments for the clergy, choral music, stained-glass win-

dows—but it preferred to choose its own saints, let its priests marry; it had the Bible translated into English and had services conducted in English along lines laid down in the Book of Common Prayer. It reduced the sacraments from seven to three (baptism, communion, and marriage). The church kept the old episcopal courts, which controlled marriages, probated wills, tried cases dealing with sexual transgressions. The old parish structure remained, and parishioners, as before, were forced to support it with tithes. The creed was "marked by moderation and studied ambiguity" but was definitely English and Protestant. "The Queen did fish for men's souls," it was said, "and had so sweet a bait that no one could escape her network." Would, she must have felt at times, that this had been true. Many believed Elizabeth had failed to purify the church sufficiently of its Catholic origins, and these Puritans by the early 1600s had become a large dissenting sect within the realm. James I threatened to harry them from the land, but for a decade the Puritans had only words to fear. Charles I determined to perform where his brother talked. His religious reforms (implemented by Archbishop Laud), tied to his political and economic "reforms," made clear that an upheaval in all sides of everyday life in England had begun. Charles I convinced those who would be called Puritans, but also many others, that the time to leave England had come.

All this the early immigrants brought with them in their heads. In the holds of their ships they packed an abundance of material things—hoes, shovels, and other familiar tools; pigs, cows, sheep, and goats; seeds from English plants; and as many personal belongings as their chests would hold. In short, they came reasonably well equipped, well prepared to start life anew. Regardless of who they were, why they came, or where they settled, most shared one goal—to transform the wilderness into an England overseas, or rather, that part of England they had known. What they found made that goal harder to achieve than expected.

What They Found

Any literate man interested in migrating to America could, by 1630 when thousands were pouring in, have collected a good-sized library of books and pamphlets about the land. Accounts had streamed in from Virginia since 1607. Captain John Smith had published a description of the region he named New England in 1614. The Pilgrims had sent back graphic reports since 1620, when they settled in at Plymouth. But however much an emigrant had read or heard firsthand from those who had returned, what he found in America seldom jibed with what he had expected to find.

According to William Bradford, the Pilgrims faced "a hideous and desolate wilderness, full of wild beasts and wild men." With those words he created a myth that will not die. Wherever they landed along the American coast, none of the first settlers had to confront a forbidding wilderness—except in their minds. (Only later as they moved inland did they have to deal with a true wilderness.) The Indians for centuries had periodically burned over the land to make it easier to hunt game or to clear it for cultivation. John Smith's tours around Chesapeake Bay in 1607 revealed innumerable stretches of open fields, some up to two hundred acres, all cultivated by Indians. Later, coasting the New England shore, he again counted scores of Indian villages surrounded by cultivated spaces, and "many isles planted with corn." The Pilgrims, coming six years after him, landed at the foot of a hillside cleared of trees and on which they planted corn, wheat, peas, and barley the following spring.

The wild men that lurked in the forests were few in New England, for the tribes there had been devastated by smallpox caught from European fishermen. (William Cronon holds that "chicken pox seems a more likely cause," but regardless of what disease prevailed it was of European origin and "its effects are well documented.") When the Pilgrims landed at Plymouth two of the few surviving Indians came out to greet them. Both spoke English, and in the months ahead did much to make the strangers at home in a new world. "Many ways hath their advice and endeavor been advantageous to us," one man said, "they being our first instructors for the planting of their Indian corn, by teaching us to cull out the finest seed, to observe the fittest season, to keep distance for holes and fit measure for hills, to worm it, and weed it, to prune it, and dress it as occasion requires." The Indians Virginia settlers met, perhaps eight thousand in number, were a more substantial danger, but fifteen years elapsed before the first major attack and another twenty before the second. During the peaceful intervals these Indians, too, helped to feed the colonists and taught them to adapt old customs to a new environment.

Others present in the new world also helped to ease the hardships of settling in. The first tobacco grown in Virginia came from purloined Spanish seed, and the technique of slowly drying the leaves under shaded roofs to produce a milder smoke also came from the Spanish. Contacts with the French—they founded Quebec in 1608, two years after Jamestown—were slight, but at least once, in 1630, they dropped off a consignment of goats in Boston. The Dutch had settled New Amsterdam in 1609, and their ships cruised up and down the coast, landing slaves in Virginia and provisions in New England— thirty-four sheep on one visit, thirty horses on another.

Bradford to the contrary, many settlers found an "earthly paradise" in America. The abundance of the flora and fauna was awesome. Persimmons, a fruit new to the colonists, grew like ropes of onions and "the branches very often break down by the mighty weight of the fruits." Wild strawberries carpeted many of the burned-over glades. In the spring "herrings come up in such abundance into their brooks and fords to spawn that it is almost impossible to ride through without treading on them." Huge turkeys ran in flocks of four and five hundred. Migrating ducks blotted out the sun when they rose from a pond and made "a rushing and vibration of the air like a great storm coming through the trees." But it was one thing to be in the midst of a paradise, another to enjoy what it offered. Few of the early settlers knew how to use a gun and nearly all arrived drained of energy by the long voyage. "Though there be fish in the sea," said John Smith, "fowls in the air, and beasts in the woods, their bounds are so large, they so wild, and we so weak and ignorant, we cannot much trouble them."

Most of the colonists found the new world less strange than expected. They met no new diseases here; all those that would strike them down originated in Europe. (To help in a further but unpleasant way to make the new world less strange, the settlers brought along with their familiar diseases familiar pests —the black fly, the cockroach, the gray rat, and the seeds of weeds unknown in America.) Neither the climate nor the land differed radically from what they had known in England, or so it seemed at first. Winters were colder in New England and summers hotter in the Chesapeake region, but the variances seemed tolerable. The rolling countryside of New England resembled areas from which many had emigrated. Even the salt marshes of the Chesapeake area, filled with "infectious bogs and muddy creeks and lakes," duplicated parts of England, although admittedly "the most unsound and most unhealthy parts."

Settlers did find three things that distinguished America from England—an abundance of wood, countless fast-running streams, and limitless vacant land—each of which would have a marked effect on their everyday lives. Wood in England by the early years of the seventeenth century had become a precious commodity. Forests had vanished into planks for ships— it took over twenty-five hundred trees to build an oceangoing vessel—into charcoal to fire forges and furnaces, and into a host of other commercial enterprises, all of which inflated over 100 percent the price of firewood for the plain people. In America the settler who had shivered through a damp English winter found a "good living for those that love good fires." A man with but "fifty acres of land may afford to give more wood for timber and fire, as good as the world yields, than many noblemen in England can afford to do." Trees provided more than warmth for the body and flames to cook by. They could be harvested. "Wood grows so fast at every man's door," one man said, "that after it has been cut down it will in seven years' time grow up again from seed to substantial firewood; and in eighteen or twenty years 'twill come to be very good board timber." The first cash crops that Jamestown and Plymouth sent home were shiploads of lumber.

The innumerable streams that rolled down from inland hills and twisted through the coastlands made distant forests accessible. The streams affected daily life in other ways. At a time when all England still sawed wood by hand, sawmills driven by waterpower proliferated up and down the coast. The streams also served as liquid highways and drew settlers into a wilderness where lay boundless miles of vacant land. Land reachable by water combined to encourage dispersion, which in turn weakened the tight hold English village life had on the early settlers. Though the colonists were wedded to their old ways of life "like a snail to his shell," wood, water, and land worked together slowly to transform the Englishman into something he did not plan on—a new breed of man.

2

THE TOWN · THE COUNTY · SOMETHING DIFFERENT

The Town

WHAT they found did not necessarily determine the way they lived. Much depended on when they came, where they went, and especially who *they* were. Those who went to New England edged toward middle age—many, if not most, were in their thirties or early forties. Age made them all the more determined to preserve a way of life known back home. Nearly all were married, with a servant or two in tow. They had been screened to exclude the "disruptive or obstinate" but to include craftsmen, physicians, midwives, ministers, and other useful people. The chosen were those who appeared devout and were deemed able to "shape the wilderness into useful space." They were to a large extent a cross section of English life; gentlemen, unlike elsewhere, led the great migration into New England.

They crossed the ocean in groups, often as members of dissenting congregations who were familiar with one another and further bound together by an eagerness to worship God as they pleased. They came expecting to stay and were called, appropriately, "planters." They erected towns—known elsewhere in America as townships—and within the towns villages resembling those known at home. No two New England towns or the villages within them were identical. They varied in time through the seventeenth century and according to the backgrounds of those who planted them. The way inhabitants farmed, the houses they built, the way they talked and dressed and governed themselves varied so much that to some it seemed as though they had come from different nations. In some towns prevailed the open-field system, where the community farmed plots of land in common, planting together, harvesting together. In others the closed-field system ruled; inhabitants received holdings they could manage as they wished. A minority within a town forced to accept agrarian customs that contradicted those they had known could resolve frustration by "hiving out"—always in a group—to some unsettled spot elsewhere, and there recreate a way of life they were at ease with.

Despite the diverse character of New England towns, some general remarks can be made about how they were created, laid out, and governed. As a rule in the early years of settlement, the central government of a New England colony assigned the site for a new town. It dispensed the land to groups; individual families or "outlivers" were rarely allowed to squat on a spot of their choosing. An average site was parceled out to thirty or forty heads of households, which gave the town at the start a population of between 150 and 200 inhabitants. Every town group contained an inner core of colonists who had known one another in England or in some previous American settlement. If a "stranger" were invited to join the group, he held good credentials—wealth or family prestige, one or the other hopefully accompanied with decorum or devoutness, or a special skill such as blacksmithing or carpentry. During the early years of settlement, groups tried to ease the enervating effort to put down roots by choosing sites previously cultivated by Indians. If they found such a spot, the central government insisted that the Indians be compensated for their loss. That done —often, however, through chicanery—it formally deeded the site to the group and settlement could begin. Towns varied greatly in size, from several hundred square miles to a small unit of some thirty square miles. The average size was slightly over one hundred square miles.

The core of the town lay in the village, and the village, like a typical one in England, stretched along a single street. The street broadened midway to make room for a green where the meetinghouse would stand and where later a burial ground would be marked by headstones. The greens then hardly resembled those seen in New England villages today. Then cows grazed on them and the local militia trained there. "Continual trampling left most greens anything but grass covered," John Stilgoe notes; "most looked like wide, muddy paddocks."

The narrow strips of house lots that flanked the street kept neighbors close, within walking distance of each other and the meetinghouse. The strips varied in size but were large enough to hold a garden, a small orchard, and enough pasture for the family's cow or two when the town herdsman brought them back to be penned up for the night. Each planter owned outright, in fee simple, his village lot and the land assigned to him elsewhere in the town. He could sell or bequeath his holdings to whom he wished as long as the town found the new owner an acceptable citizen.

The size of a householder's holdings depended on his social status, and that in turn hinged on several things. Wealth played a part, as well as education and family background. But a man of character and intelligence, elected year after year to important town posts, could hold high rank regardless of his lack of wealth or pedigree. In subtle ways lost to posterity, everyone knew his place in society. Families of low status got lots at the extreme ends of the street. The upper class had the choice spots near the center, and all others were scattered through a "twilight zone."

Every town was in fact "a little commonwealth." In the beginning the central government tried to create a homogeneous colony by regulating the way of life in all towns. It defined the "just price" a craftsman could charge for his product, fixed wages, outlawed usurious interest rates. Its sumptuary legislation sought to control the people's private lives, forbidding profane language, lavish dress, excessive drinking. The towns balked at outside interference, much as they had in England when the Stuarts tried similar intrusions in town life, and within a decade all had become their own masters. This did not mean the end of control over people's daily lives. Matters handled by ecclesiastical courts in England, from marriage to sexual perversion, were now dealt with by local magistrates, who in New England "in all things [had] the like power that justices of the peace hath in England for reformation of abuses and punishing of offenders." Regulations were as detailed and even more extensive than those known in English villages. The towns chose their own ministers, controlled the local militia, appointed the village herdsman. A fallen tree that blocked a roadway, a shoddy fence, an unpenned dog in heat—all came within the purview of local leaders. Numerous elected officials—selectmen, fence-viewers, highway overseers, the constable, the militia officer—ran the town on a day-to-day basis, but every planter was expected to show up at town meetings, to vote on every issue, and to accept any public office (unpaid) he was elected to.

Despite the variety of early New England towns, John Demos's comments on East Hampton, Long Island, seem to fit for the life lived within most of them.

> All things considered, the life of the town was *corporate* to a remarkable degree. The citizens were indeed a body, each one integrated into part of the larger whole. Experience came to them in, and by, and through the group; literally and figuratively, they lived in each other's presence. Their houses lay huddled together along a single street. Their field-lots were scattered in every direction—two acres here, four acres there, but always among a bevy of neighbors. They

accepted common tasks and they shared both good and bad fortune. They worked together, they worshipped together, governed together.

The corporate ideal never expanded much beyond the boundaries of New England. There, outwardly, it appeared to survive well into the eighteenth century. People continued to hive out in groups, and wherever they went they recreated a village with the meetinghouse at its center. But the reality seldom matched the ideal of a village where every member's welfare was interwoven into the whole community. Settlers insisted on dispersing out from the center. Massachusetts in 1635 ordered all town residents not to settle more than a half mile from the meetinghouse; five years later it had to repeal the flouted law. Men wanted land—"Land! Land!" Increase Mather complained in 1676, "has been the idol of many in New England"—and accessible, free land soon led them away from the village, beyond the sound of the church bell, into the wilderness. Most resettled within the town's expansive boundaries, and until they created hamlets that eventually became villages they were denizens of the forest.

The County

The Chesapeake region presents a different story. When Massachusetts Bay began, it resembled a normal society to the extent that the family predominated and the number of men and women were nearly balanced. Virginia began, and for nearly four decades remained, an abnormal society. In 1624, seventeen years after the first settlement, there were only 244 females, children included, out of a population of 1,292. Mostly single men came—"adventurers" as the London Company rightly called them. They cared little about religion. They were young, ambitious, and competitive, lured to America by the hope of quick wealth. Few planned to live out their lives there.

Many, however, did, for the death rate was appalling. During the first decade of settlement at least two thirds of the immigrants died, and the statistics did not improve until the 1640s. The Indians, a negligible danger in New England, killed nearly a thousand settlers in two massive raids in the Chesapeake, one in 1622, the other in 1644.

The worst sides of English life flourished in a brutal, self-centered society that lacked communal bonds of any kind. Manners and morals collapsed. During the "starving time," some "fed on the corpses of dead men, and one who had gotten insatiable, out of custom to that food, could not be restrained until such time as he was executed for it." Excessive drinking prevailed. Community cooperation and restraints found in the English village vanished. Every man looked out for himself. In the winter of 1631–32, one entrepreneur collected two thousand bushels of corn in Virginia and sold them to New Englanders while his brethren at home wanted for food. The ideal of the commonwealth, "in which the interest of every part would be harmoniously subordinated to the larger interest of the whole society," never appeared.

The fault lay only partly with the character of the settlers. The land itself and the early success of tobacco as a cash crop combined to assure the end of village life. The settlers' "greediness after great quantities of tobacco causeth them after five or six years continually to remove and therefore neither build good homes, fence their grounds, or plant any orchards." The peculiar characteristics of Chesapeake Bay, unique along the Atlantic coast, encouraged this apparently shiftless use of the land and steady dispersion of the settlers. A shoreline of some two thousand miles of the enormous bay (which stretched nearly two hundred miles in length) could be reached by seventeenth-century seagoing vessels, and most of the 150 or so rivers, creeks, branches, and other middling streams that fed into it were navigable by the same ships. One visitor found that "most houses are built near some landing place, so that any thing may be delivered to a gentleman there from London, Bristol, etc., with less trouble and cost than to one living five miles in the country in England." This "well-watered" land as much as the tobacco farmer's so-called greed helped to kill village life in Virginia. A hogshead of tobacco weighed nearly half a ton, far too heavy and costly to haul overland to a market center, but little trouble or expense in a country where a to-bacco ship could tie up at the edge of one's farm. Every farm, "even the most remote," a visitor remarked, "is no more than one or one hundred and fifty feet from a 'crik,' and the people are thus enabled not only to pay their visits in their canoes but to do all their freight carrying by the same means."

By 1640 a pattern of life alien to the English experience had taken shape in the Chesapeake. Authorities chafed at the trans-formation. "For how is it possible," one of them asked, "to govern a people so dispersed; especially such [rabble] as for the most part are sent over? How can they repair to divine service except every plantation have a minister? How can we raise soldiers to go upon the enemy or workmen for public employ-ments, without weakening them too much, or undoing them by drawing them from their labors? Whereas if we had planted together we could have borne out one another's labors and given both strength and beauty to the colony." In short, as Edmund Morgan puts the question, how, "without proximity to promote a sense of community," could the colonists "bind themselves together by imposing on each other a strict standard of behavior?"

The central government, as in Massachusetts, tried to restore English standards of rectitude and behavior. The statutes that poured from Virginia's House of Burgesses differed little from those issued by the Massachusetts General Court. They sought to dominate all sides of settlers' lives. They limited the amount of tobacco a farmer could plant, demanded that he also "plant and tend two acres of corn," that he brand his cattle. If he failed to build a sturdy fence at least four and a half feet high, any

damage sustained "by hogs, goats, or cattle shall be his own loss
and detriment." Laws regulated the treatment of servants and
Indians, fixed physicians' fees and laborers' wages. Sundays
were not to be profaned, and every settler "having no lawful
excuse to be absent" must attend church regularly, "upon pen-
alty of being fined fifty pounds of tobacco." The lack of a minister gave no excuse for nonattendance; in his stead "a sober
person of good life" should be chosen to read the divine service.
Marriages must be solemnized by a minister and, as in England,
the banns published "according to the prescription in *The Common Book of Prayer.*"

It was up to the governor to enforce these regulations, but as
the settlers fanned out farther and farther, distance from the
center made that impossible. As in New England, authority
devolved downward—there to the town, here to the county.
The county's justices of the peace together with the parish
vestry—often composed of the same men—took over local government, which now focused on the county seat, an artificial
village which stirred alive only occasionally through the year
when the court sat, when elections were held, and after the
tobacco fleet had cleared for England and farmers met to pay
and collect debts.

The church's voice became a faint echo of what it had been.
Much that the clergy had done at home civilians now did. Wills
were filed with the county clerk. Births and deaths and land
titles were recorded—if at all—in his office. The marriage license, devised in place of the banns to alert a widespread community of an intended event, was issued from his office. Cases
once handled by ecclesiastical courts were now dealt with by
the parish vestry, which also assumed the right to hire and fire
ministers. The multitude of duties of the English justice of the
peace revived in Virginia, but without a close-knit community
to sustain him decisions were often flouted.

On paper the Chesapeake county by midcentury seemed as
well-regulated as the New England town. The facts were other-

wise. A strong sense of community refused to surface in the region. Citizens continued to do much as they wished. Their values, their standards of behavior were their own, rarely restrained by community pressure or inhibited by laws on the books. Religion had little effect on their lives. They made slight effort to educate the upcoming generation. No colonywide institution, not the church, not the legislature, had the respect or authority to promote a sense of common purpose among the plain people.

Something Different

The Chesapeake settlers shaped the wilderness into useful space one way, New Englanders another. Both regions were settled by Englishmen and drew heavily on English traditions as they adapted to America. They sought whenever possible to conserve rather than innovate. Something different happened in the Middle Colonies, where an ethnic and religious diversity of settlers made it difficult to know what to conserve, what to discard. For instance, the Dutch along the Hudson Valley and later the Germans in Pennsylvania marked time by the New Style (Gregorian) calendar, while the English clung to the Old Style (Julian) calendar; a difference of ten days between calendars made it difficult to know when to celebrate holidays, Easter especially. How was one to conduct business when the Germans were accustomed to talers, the Dutch to guilders, the English to pounds, shillings, and pence? In Europe, governments established—that is, protected—a particular church within its boundaries. In America it was relatively easy with a homogeneous population to determine what church should prevail in a colony, as the Congregational church did in New England and the Anglican church in Virginia. But what church could the New Netherlands establish when the settlers consisted of Dutch, French, English, and Jewish planters? Daniel Pastorius, a Mennonite from the Rhine Valley, crossed to Pennsylvania in

1683 aboard what he called a Noah's Ark of religious faiths—
Roman Catholics, Lutherans, Calvinists, Anabaptists, and Quakers. How, out of this diversity, did one reproduce an old way of
life? Timothy L. Smith has put the problem well:

> But how did one create community, when the only kind he had
> known seemed a natural inheritance, not a human contrivance? The
> pattern of life in the European village and town had been marvel-
> ously intricate. Habits so deeply ingrained as to require little con-
> scious thought regulated word, work, and worship. To each person
> and family belonged usually a status in the neighborhood, and a set
> of duties and privileges to fit it. To fashion new and equally secure
> relationships in the American wilderness seemed a task beyond
> mere human capacity.

William Penn, as he planned for Pennsylvania, saw this problem
and a larger one—how to create out of a mélange of settlers of
diverse ethnic and religious backgrounds "a commonwealth
founded on the principle of brotherly love . . . which would
stand above the differences in religion that every settlement
was bound to display." His solution, although it ultimately
failed, was ingenious.

Penn discarded the notion of reproducing the English village
in his colony. Well over a half century of American history told
him it could not be done in a colony that welcomed people from
all parts of Europe. In its stead he conceived the hamlet. Land
would be surveyed into townships of five thousand acres, a
space large enough to support ten families who shared similar
backgrounds. Individual holdings would be carved out of the
township into giant pie-like slices. Settlers would build their
homes at the tip of each slice, and every family would be within
walking distance of one another and whatever church they
chose to erect.

(Before moving on, let it be noted that one scholar argues
against much that has just been said. He writes: "Don't think it
was really half a century of New World experience that con-

vinced Penn not to insist upon the village model in Pennsylvania. His whole plan of government was based upon decidedly English ideals, and he didn't know that much more about America otherwise. He really was anything but a practical man. Nor was the hamlet an original creation of Penn or of America: it was the predominant form in parts of northern and western England and throughout Scotland [the farmtown] and Ireland." Let us now proceed.)

What looked fine on paper failed to materialize. Settlers decided they did not like the long trek from the hamlet out to the rim of their farms. They soon built houses within or near the center of their slice of land, thus spreading farmsteads as far apart as those in the Chesapeake. But the hamlet remained, a cluster of buildings that perhaps held a house and shop for a blacksmith and possibly others for a carpenter, a cooper, or a wheelwright, but for sure it held a church, a place to gather for a drink, and above all a store. European travelers found it hard to describe the store for those at home. A Frenchman discarded *magasin* and *boutique* as inadequate, for "neither of these words conveys its meaning completely, according to the peculiar character, object, and use of store in America; and especially in places thinly inhabited. . . . A store is a shop or place where all kinds of commodities intended for consumption are to be found and sold by retail; nothing is excluded from it." The goods for sale varied from pots and pans to spices, coffee, tea, buttons, stockings, shoes, hats, and various bolts of cloth, but the storekeeper chose his stock to fit the needs and desires of those who came to the hamlet.

But the hamlet's few craftsmen and its general store, as it came to be called, could not handle all the surrounding area's needs. They served an area too small to support mills to grind grain and saw lumber and merchants to aid in marketing produce. Settlers along the Delaware could reach the port town of Philadelphia by water, but planters in the interior could get there only by land. Travel by land was costly and slow; a loaded wagon could move no more than thirty miles a day. Intermediate ports of call were needed and that need created market towns, similar to those in England—Lancaster, York, and later Carlisle to the west of Philadelphia; Allentown, Bethlehem, and Easton to the north. The lack of a network of waterways as in the Chesapeake led to the building of a network of roads that led like spokes of a wheel to a market-town hub, thence by other spokes to Philadelphia.

Penn was a practical visionary but even he did not perceive that the ethnic variety of people already in the Delaware Valley, added to those drawn from Europe and all parts of Great Britain by his promise of religious toleration and easy acquisition of land, would create the first truly innovative society in America. Outwardly the settlement resembled what had gone before. As in New England migrants came mostly in family groups, and they also came as planters, expecting to live permanently in their new world. Philadelphia, though a planned city laid out in the form of a gridiron of great squares to create what Penn called "a green country town," was also designed like Boston and New York as a port town that gathered in staple crops from the hinterland. The county, as in the Chesapeake, would become the key political unit the plain people would relate to. The word *neighborhood* would take on a new meaning, as it already had elsewhere in America. In England, whether one lived in a village, a market town, or in London, one's visible neighbors comprised one's neighborhood. In America by the time Penn's colony emerged the word had come to mean that area one could reach in an easy day's walk or, after the horse became common, an easy day's ride.

Superficial resemblances aside, the settlement of the Delaware Valley and Pennsylvania in particular presented something new to America. First, the swiftness of settlement was like nothing that had occurred before, not even in the great migrations into New England and the Chesapeake. In 1682, when the flood began, only a few hundred people lived in the Delaware

Valley. Three years later there were over eight thousand, more than in the Chesapeake after three decades of settlement. By the end of the century some twenty-five thousand had spread up and down the banks of the Delaware and westward into the interior. This great inrush of people called for haste in clearing the land and building homes. As John Stilgoe puts it, "Speed, not quality of product, dictated techniques and form." Planters had to borrow from where and from whom they could if they were to shape the wilderness into useful space.

Fortunately, they had much to borrow from. The Chesapeake taught them how to open up a forest by girdling trees and how to encircle their holdings with easily erected snake fences. The Swedes brought the log cabin from home. New England and the Chesapeake ignored the innovation and tediously constructed clapboard-sided houses similar to those they had known. Penn's settlers accepted the log cabin at once and lived snugly within them until they had time to build something more substantial. The Swedes also taught English newcomers how to use the ax, a tool many were unfamiliar with. "They will cut down a tree and cut him up when down sooner than two men could saw him, and rend him into planks or what they please only with an ax and wooden wedge," a contemporary said. "A Swede will fell twelve of the biggest oaks in a day."

Germans and Swedes together brought from home new ways to convert the wilderness more swiftly into livable, useful space. When a newcomer arrived in the neighborhood those around gathered to help erect his log cabin. Later when he needed help in clearing a field, the neighborhood gathered again for a log-rolling and "stump-pulling frolic." Autumn butchering, a family affair elsewhere, became "one of the greatest fete days of the year for Pennsylvania Germans," Stevenson Whitcomb Fletcher reports.

> It usually occurred late in November. Neighbors of both sexes were invited. They arrived about four o'clock in the morning to find huge

log fires already burning and hogs and beef cattle butchered, scalded and hung up. The day was spent cutting up the meat, making sausage, rendering the lard, making scrapple, and smoking the hams and bacons over fires of green hickory chips. . . . At night after partaking of *schnatz betz* (rye whisky) all go home carrying with them as much sausage and fresh meat as needed.

Another community event introduced by the Germans was the barn raising. After the farmer has dug the foundation, laid the walls, and prepared the joists, studding, rafters and other needed lumber, "he *I-lauds* (invites) his friends and neighbors to come to the *curb-blocking* (raising) and with their united strength and labor the whole skeleton is erected." Meanwhile the ladies have set the dinner table. "Here will be found metzel soup, hamburg sausage, *wurst, sauerkraut,* potatoes, *snitz and knep,* innumerable kinds of pies, cakes, cider and apples, apple butter, *smeer case,* all kinds of jams and jellies, all blended in a mass on the same table." The day ends with a dance on the newly laid threshing floor. Within a few years of settlement the Germans were plowing cleared fields while colonists elsewhere were still grubbing out tree stumps and turning up the soil with hoes. Also, while others continued to let their livestock roam, the Germans had fenced theirs in, built barns to house them in winter, and were using the manure to fertilize their fields. The carts New England used to haul produce to market would not do in Pennsylvania, where distances between hamlets, market towns, and Philadelphia were great by European standards. German craftsmen designed a deep-bellied wagon—the Conestoga wagon, later called the prairie schooner—that could haul four times the load of an English cart. To pull these "moving houses," the Germans bred horses that looked like behemoths to outlanders accustomed to the sturdy but small English horses. Other German craftsmen produced a new gun for America—the rifle, known through colonial history as the Pennsylvania rifle (largely through the renown of Daniel Boone, born and bred in Pennsylvania) but later called the Kentucky rifle.

The peculiar mixture of people and religions encouraged by William Penn made Pennsylvania from the beginning less tied to the English past than were other parts of early America. The lateness of settlement also allowed it to draw on the experience of two generations of colonists who had adapted old customs to a new world. Although formally a colony for less than two decades when the seventeenth century ended, Pennsylvania's settlers would have agreed with what Henry Adams wrote much later—"the conceptions of life were different" in this unique new-world province.

3

THE FARM

I T EXAGGERATES to say that seventeenth-century America invented that dispersed, relatively isolated agricultural unit called a farm. It existed in parts of Scotland and in southeastern England. Nonetheless, the typical English yeoman's life differed considerably from the American farmer's. It wove inextricably into the village where often he had been born and reared. He seldom lived beyond the sound of the church bell. A short walk brought him the companionship of the local pub or tavern. A host of craftsmen—sawyers, blacksmiths, coopers, carpenters, wheelwrights—lay near at hand when needed. Such close community ties all but vanished with the appearance of the American farm. The farmer and his family lived semi-secluded lives, the nearest neighbors often no closer than a half mile or so.

The Chesapeake region, without forethought, created the first farms. The enticement of abundant land that abutted on the bay and the countless streams that fed into it drew the settlers outward along the vast shoreline soon after the tobacco bonanza began. So much has been made of the village life of New England that many forget a similar enticement of vacant land worked a similar effect in that region, only more slowly. Douglas McManis has described the process.

Many a New England farmer found the dispersed-field pattern an inconvenience, even though paths soon led from the village plot to all major fields. The distance separating field from village could be considerable and in order to cut down on the time spent traveling among the fields, a farmer might put up a shed for tools, animals, or drop storage at a convenient point along one of the paths. Later he might convert it into a shelter for himself and other men who worked in the neighborhood but lived in the village. Finally, he would build a substantial house for himself and family and leave the village. When farms were established on distant, newly allocated land, however, the families often migrated from the village to homestead in one step.

This occurred especially when the original settlers' children matured and parents' holdings in distant parts of the town were parceled out to them. Distance from the center loosened ties with the village, and the later generations of New England farmers came to be as nearly isolated as their counterparts in the Chesapeake region. Similar dispersions occurred in the Hudson and Delaware valleys, and by the end of the seventeenth century the American farm had become a fixed institution. Although farms differed in detail from colony to colony, all shared four characteristics: they were cut off from daily contact with the larger world; they were, up to a point, self-sustaining, they were family-run; and, by modern standards they were small.

Clearing the Ground

Once settlement moved inland beyond the sites that had been planted by Indians, the colonists faced a bleak task, so arduous that "it provided succeeding generations of Americans with one of their most forceful figures of speech denoting hard work"—clearing the ground. A settler could clear in a year no more than an acre or two, and in a lifetime he would have less than a hundred acres of cultivable land and pasture to pass on to a son. It took about a half century to carve a farm with cleared fields out of the wilderness.

Much has been made of the so-called Protestant work ethic the early settlers brought with them. It would be truer to say that the demands of clearing the ground created such an ethic. England, with its surplus of labor, was a land of underemployed people who averaged about four hours a day at their work. America might be a land rich and fat, but it asked more work than that from someone who expected to survive. "I would have no man," went one warning to emigrants, "trusting too much to the fertility of the bounds where he is to go, and too little to his own providence and industry." America might be a land of promise, but "the promise was to the diligent rather than to the adventuresome." There was wood for fires, but he must first "cut and fetch it home" before he could burn it. There was wood for housing, but he "must build his house before he would have it." In short, men had in America "all things to do, as in the beginning of the world," and one of the first things to do was clear the land.

Clearing in the Chesapeake began by girdling the trees, a technique that probably was learned from the Indians though it was known in England. "The best way we found in Virginia to spoil the woods," John Smith reported, "was first to cut a notch in the bark a hand broad round about the tree, which pull off and the tree will sprout no more and all the small boughs in a year or two will decay." Soon sunlight filtered through the withered branches and the farmer planted beneath them. New England, wedded to the past, tried at first to recreate the manicured fields known at home, chopping down trees and grubbing out stumps, but even there, as settlers moved inland, girdling became accepted. Europeans saw the expanse of deadened trees, standing like ghostly sentinels, as "very singular and dreadful," but "the savage-looking space," John Stilgoe points out, "was actually an intelligent and innovative response to providing food for family and livestock at once." After a year or so the farmer might chop down a stretch of the gray hulks and burn them. He left the stumps to rot in the field; they might remain there for a decade, for he had no way to yank them from the soil until he acquired oxen.

The Chesapeake settlers displayed their second innovative response to America in the way they fenced their lands. The need for fencing in England was not compelling, for few predatory animals roamed the countryside. Ancient hedges or wide ditches served to mark boundaries, and when those were lacking a durable post-and-rail fence was erected. Fences were obligatory in America, and they had to be "pig-tight, horse-high, and bull-strong." The Chesapeake region quickly settled on a program that called for settlers to fence in their crops and fence out their livestock, letting cattle and other domestic animals run wild in the surrounding forest. New England followed the same policy. "Every man must secure his corn and meadow against great cattle," ran a Massachusetts order in 1642, and "if any damage be done by such cattle, it shall be borne by him through whose insufficient fence the cattle did enter." Virginia called for a standard height of four and a half feet to protect crops. The legislated height in New England varied from town to town, but something close to the Virginia pattern evolved. Guilford, Connecticut, ordered its fences raised from four to four and a half feet in 1633, and Portsmouth, Rhode Island, chose the same height in 1671.

The first settlers everywhere erected some form of the post-and-rail fence—vertical posts planted in the ground with cross beams nailed to them; the Swedes substituted switches for nails. But such fences were soon abandoned in most regions; nails were costly, durable switches proved impossible to find, and the posts rotted within a few years. New England, however, despite the disadvantages, stuck to the post-and-rail fence, which to erect and maintain cost, some said, "almost as much as the land is worth." Howard S. Russell describes its laborious construction:

For posts, the farmer felled foot-thick straight-grained trees (chestnut or red cedar). These he cut to six-foot lengths and split in half; next with augur and chisel he mortised [cut a hole in] the upper portion every four to six inches. He set them in holes dug nine to ten feet apart. For rails he took much larger oak or ash trees, cut their boles into eleven-foot lengths, and split each length so as to make eight or sixteen rails. Their ends were then slipped into the mortises of one post after another, the holes filled and made solid.

The New England fence revealed a farmer committed to his holding for life, and also one who found it hard to adapt to a unique environment. Others saw there was no time to build things that would last forever. If a man and his family were to survive, haste was needed to clear the land and fence it in. The Chesapeake region designed the fence most of America adopted, the split-rail zigzag fence, which, as its use moved northward, also came to be called the snake or worm fence from its serpentine lines. Split rails were crisscrossed atop one another in a Z formation that required only a slanted stake at each interlacing corner to hold them firmly in place. Europeans regarded them with contempt because they required immense quantities of wood and their twisting shape, which cut a swath ten feet wide, wasted tillable land. Such fences were in fact an imaginative innovation. They could be built quickly by unskilled hands. A man handy with an ax and wedge could cut 150 or 200 rails ten feet long from a single bole in a day, while a co-worker could during the same day convert the rails into two hundred yards of fence. They needed no postholes, yet were durable, easy to repair, and—because they could with equal ease be torn down and reassembled at another site—perfect for settlers not committed for life to a particular plot of land.

Subsistence

The farmer's work force—principally himself, his sons and wife helping out during planting and harvest seasons—limited what he could accomplish in a year. Rarely could he afford hired labor, although he might have an indentured servant or two if able to pay the cost of their passage. White labor prevailed through most of the seventeenth century. Blacks were few, even in the South, until the last decades of the seventeenth century. Estimates put the number in Virginia around three hundred in 1640 and thirty years later around two thousand out of a population of some forty thousand whites. Most of the blacks came from the Spanish Indies or directly from Africa and were of small use to a farmer with little time to spare in directing an untrained man who spoke a strange tongue.

His tools further limited the farmer. In the beginning and for a long time thereafter they were the simplest—shovels, spades, hoes, and mattocks, all generally made of wood with the cutting edges sheathed with a strip of iron. His felling ax was cumbersome, made more so because few of the early settlers were accustomed to using it. The head was made of brittle iron that often cracked in cold weather, and the thin steel blade welded into it called for constant sharpening. The heavy head, with little or no poll on the dull end to counterbalance the cutting edge, made it hard for even a skilled axman to swing it without a wobble as it approached the mark. Oddly, for an instrument so crucial to hastening the settlement of America, it took more than a century for the curved-handled, nicely balanced, lightweight American ax, three times as efficient as the ax brought from England, to evolve. The same held true for the scythe, which only slowly changed from the straight-handled tool with a straight cutting bar into one with a gracefully curved blade and handle seen on small farms today.

For at least a generation most farmers worked the land with hand tools. Plows were uncommon until the 1670s, and even when plows came in they, too, were made from wood, sculptured from ash or oak usually; because their final form depended on the workman's talent no two looked alike. The late arrival of plows, which awaited the arrival of oxen and horses

powerful enough to pull them, kept all farmers imprisoned in
a pattern of garden husbandry, as opposed to field husbandry,
that lasted through most of the century. Only when the fields
had been cleared of stones and boulders in New England,
stumps and roots elsewhere, could a new form of agriculture
take shape. Meanwhile, the hoe, the shovel, and the mattock
were used to cultivate the land.

Every farmer grew corn, a miraculous plant, equally nourish-
ing to man and beast, immune to most diseases, easy to raise—
it took no more than fifty days a year of a farmer's time and
thrived in a field of girdled trees—and easy to harvest. The yield
per acre was high, about seven times that of wheat or barley.
No part of the plant went unused: the stalks served as winter
fodder for cattle, the husks to stuff mattresses, the cobs as jug
stoppers, tool handles, and the bowls of corncob pipes. Poultry
thrived on the kernels.

The settlers adopted their corn culture entirely from the
Indians. They planted when the Indians told them to—"when
the white oak leaves reach the size of a mouse's ear"—and the
way they told them, dropping several kernels in holes three or
four feet apart, later "hilling" the seedlings by scooping soil
around them for support, then fertilizing them with herring
which flooded up the streams to spawn during the late spring,
though this last technique they may have brought from England. (To keep dogs from digging up the fish, New England
farmers tied "one forepaw to the neck for forty days after planting.") The landscape of muddy fields that Rhys Isaac describes
for Virginia can be broadened to include all of colonial America
during the corn planting season: "men and women moving
through the mire, bending over about six thousand times a day,
making holes in the crowns of the hills 'with their fingers or a
small stick' for the reception of the corn seeds." When the stalks
were two or three feet high, beans and pumpkin seeds were
planted around them, Indian fashion; the stalks served as bean-
poles and gave shade to the pumpkin vines. Indians taught the

settlers how to harvest the corn, how to grind it into meal, how to preserve it through the year. The settlers also accepted most of the Indian dishes and their Indian names—such as pone, hominy, samp, and succotash—although, curiously, they refused the Indian word *maize* and persisted in calling it corn, a generic term for cereal grains in England.

The basic corn diet was supplemented with produce from the kitchen garden found behind every farmhouse. There grew vegetables the settlers had been accustomed to at home—parsnips, turnips, onions, peas, cabbage, carrots—all of which were served in traditional ways. Every farmer who planned to make his land a home and not just a way station planted an orchard not far from the house. The orchard ran mostly to apple and peach trees, fruits favored as much for their nutritive value as for the fine cider, applejack, and brandy produced from them.

The early settlers brought pigs, chickens, and goats from home, but the hog quickly became the staple meat in everyone's diet. Hogs were excellent foragers, able to live on what they found in the woods. (The saying "root hog or die" came to be a favorite among settlers seeking to survive in the wilderness.) Wolves took their toll of the free-running hogs but seldom in the vicinity of a tusked old boar. When killing time came, all the hog was used, as another saying went, but the squeal: the intestines for sausage skins, the bladder to hold lard, the long hair from the tail to sew buckskins. The meat from four good-sized hogs salted down in barrels could carry a family through the winter. If for some reason the family saw the bottom of the pork barrel before spring arrived, it knew it faced a thin diet in the weeks ahead.

All the colonists' domestic animals were brought from England—the Indians had none to offer but dogs—often in the first incoming ships. They brought not only swine, chickens, and goats, but sheep, horses, and cattle as well. One New Englander, no doubt better off than most, listed in his inventory in 1635 sixty-four goats, ninety-two sheep, twenty-two horses, and fifty-eight cattle. Apparently he, like most, raised few chickens; they remained unpopular until toward the end of the century when someone discovered they thrived on corn kernels.

Goats were welcomed at first for several reasons: they were easy to transport to America, they fed on almost anything, and they provided milk and cheese; but when their voracious appetites pushed them into kitchen gardens and loosely fenced fields they lost favor with settlers. Sheep were welcomed mainly for their wool, but they, too, had drawbacks. They were fussy eaters who demanded grassy meadows, of which there were then few, they bit close to the ground and left little for other livestock to feed on, they were docile and easy prey for wolves, and they required shepherds round the clock. Horses imported from England were too small to be of much use except for riding in a land where there were few roads to ride along. They came to be valued only later when they were exported to the West Indies to work the cane mills there.

Cattle and swine received a lasting welcome through the century up and down the coast. Both provided not only sustenance but also a cash income, especially cattle. Indeed, cattle raising can be called the first major industry for all American farmers. Plymouth survived its early trials nicely by selling off its surplus cattle to newcomers in Massachusetts Bay. "It is a wonder," one New Englander said in 1660, "to consider how many thousand neat beasts and hogs are yearly killed and have been for many years past for provision in the country and sent abroad to supply Newfoundland, Barbados and Jamaica." In the Chesapeake cattle were "the most secure commodity of wealth," more valuable than land. They were sold to supply meat for tobacco ships that often had to wait weeks to gather their cargoes. They were exported both live and butchered to the West Indies. Cattle rather than land were often willed to children orphaned by a father's death. The legal guardian was compensated with the male and the children got title to the female cattle. "The acquisition of the male cattle produced a lucrative compensation for bringing the youngster up," Edmund Morgan notes. "Men competed for the right." Cattle ran wild in the South; they were fenced in on farms to the north or, notably in New England, tended by a hired cowherd in the villages. Rustling early on became a problem, and everywhere the cattle were branded, usually by a personalized notching in the ear, "a relatively insensible member of the body and of practically no utility to any other than the beast itself," Wesley Frank Craven remarks. "Earmarks—nicks, slits, croppings, underbits, overbits, and holes—placed on either or both ears offered for the convenience of the community an amazing number of combinations." Brands were registered with the town clerk in New England, the county clerk elsewhere.

Nature, as with farmers everywhere, ruled the American farmer's life, but it was a nature that differed from the one known in England. Wheat blast could ruin a string of harvests, as it did in New England during the 1660s. The jimsonweed—a corruption of "Jamestown weed"—could drive cattle berserk and turn men who unwisely sampled it into "natural fools [who] would have wallowed in their own excrement if they had not been prevented." Pests of all sorts abounded. Some, like gnats, mosquitoes, bedbugs, roaches, and the hordes of flies that blackened uncovered food in an instant, only annoyed man and beast. Others like the tobacco fly and worms could, unless promptly swept away, ruin entire crops. Caterpillars sometimes rolled in like an invading army and devoured meadows of grass and fields of barley, corn, and wheat. The farmer had to deal with new predators—wolves, wildcats, and black bears—all native to America. Wolves presented the greatest danger. They preyed especially on cattle that roamed abroad, for they were easier to kill than the fleet deer. Every colony offered bounties for them. The intrepid raccoon, another native, was endowed with a delicate palate; it waited until a week or so before the corn ripened, then swooped in at night to feast until contented. Passenger pigeons, which migrated about the time corn ripened, were a worse threat. They were known as "maize thieves" and when they alit in a field could flatten the whole crop in an instant.

The farmer expected and accepted nature's excesses—too much or too little rain or snow, drought, hailstones as large as a fist—but the extremes in America swung a wider arc than he had counted on. The thunderstorm, the three-day northeaster, and the hurricane were phenomena new to him. The first recorded new-world hurricane (noted with astonishment) struck Massachusetts in 1635 and "blew down many hundreds of trees, . . . overthrew some houses, drove ships from their anchors." Others followed intermittently throughout the century. A Chesapeake region accustomed to mild winters had one in 1672–73 that killed half the unsheltered cattle of Virginia. Regardless of where a man settled in America a farmer's life remained as always a precarious existence—either feast or famine.

Two Kinds of Farms

Farms in the North differed from region to region. In New England the fields were edged by stone walls as well as post-and-rail fences. (The walls were too low to be useful as fences; they served to mark borders and as a neat way to arrange rocks rolled from the fields.) As a traveler moved down the coast, the snake fence appeared and the log cabin supplanted the clapboard cottage. Still, by the end of the century northern farms had much in common. Regardless of the house a family lived in, it was rude, small, and unpainted (paint was expensive and had to be imported), and it stood starkly in an unshaded clearing. Shingles, which in most places had come to replace thatched roofs, rotted in the shade. Moreover, a tree close by might fall during a storm and crush the house. However, a fruit tree or two usually stood on a spot where a privy had once been before it had to be moved. A well, if there was one, usually lay uphill from the privy, for the settlers sensed a connection between disease and polluted water.

The house generally faced south, and in front of it, shielded from northern winds, lay the kitchen garden, and farther away the orchard. Behind the house but far enough away not to be endangered by sparks from the house's chimney, sat the barn. Early settlers had been accustomed in England to a small cow-house for milking and another rude building where they threshed grain. Combining them into a single structure was an American innovation. Barn designs differed throughout the North but generally they served similar purposes—to house the livestock through winters much colder than those known in England, to store fodder, thresh grain, and keep tools. Also, as Robert Blair St. George discreetly puts it, they "seem to have found frequent use as arenas for antisocial behavior and for aggressions that could . . . not find expression in the yeoman's house." On older, more substantial farms there might also be a corncrib, pigsty, woodshed, and one or two other outbuildings —a chicken coop, wagon shed, or smokehouse.

Most northern farms even at the end of the century were small, seldom more than fifty acres of tillable land and meadows. But changes had occurred through the century. The dismal sight of girdled trees was giving way to cleared fields. Plows with oxen to pull them were appearing on the landscape, and most farmers owned a horse or two for traveling about the neighborhood. Everywhere diversified farming prevailed. No farm could be called self-sufficient—all at some time during the year had to call on the outside world for material goods of one sort or another—and few produced enough to carry a family much above the subsistence level. Among northern farmers, James A. Henretta has said,

> there was little innovative, risk-taking behavior; there was no deter-
> mined pursuit of profit. Indeed, the account books of these farm

families indicate that they invariably chose the security of diversified production rather than hire labor to produce more wheat or to specialize in milk production. Economic gain was important to these men and women, yet it was not their dominant value. It was subordinate to (or encompassed by) two other goals: the yearly subsistence and the long-run financial security of the family unit.

Once the traveler had passed beyond the Delaware Valley and crossed into Chesapeake country he came upon farms that resembled nothing seen before either in America or Europe. Rarely did he find anything about them to praise. They were shoddy, carelessly managed, almost disgustingly shabby. Carville V. Earle reprimands travelers and historians who denigrate these tobacco farms and defends the dilapidated landscape of the Chesapeake. "In a mobile agricultural system," he writes, "the deterioration of buildings and land was integral to the functioning of the system. Unkempt old fields restored fertility. In stump-littered tobacco fields, laborers hoed around the hulks and thus saved the expense of rooting them out. Tobacco houses were semi-permanent facilities relocated with shifting fields. The planters either abandoned the old tobacco house or dismantled it for reconstruction near the new field. . . . Tidewater landscapes, atrophied and in disarray, sacrificed esthetics for economics and ecology."

The planter's eagerness to produce a large cash crop left him little time for other sides of farm life. His house remained a hovel. He tended to neglect the orchard and sometimes even the kitchen garden. The tobacco and corn planting seasons coincided, which often meant that he failed to plant enough corn to carry the family through the year. He knew that tobacco wore out the soil in three or four years, yet he failed to fertilize his fields. Not out of ignorance, however, but because his livestock grazed in the woods and, more important, because merchants told him that fertilized fields produced a leaf that tasted of manure. Those who charged him with laziness failed to note that he grew the most demanding crop produced in colonial America.

Work began in late February or early March when the seeds were planted in flats. They had to be closely watched as they sprouted, covered with brush or straw to protect them from late frosts, then uncovered to catch the sun again. The seedlings were transplanted in early April by the same laborious technique used to plant corn. One man tended some ten thousand plants which covered about three acres. Unlike corn or other grains the plants had to be closely cared for through the summer—swept clean of worms and other pests, pruned, hoed free of weeds. The plants were cut in August, carried to the tobacco shed, and hung from horizontal stakes. There the shaded leaves dried slowly, wafted by breezes that flowed through the open ends and loose-jointed sides of the shed. They hung there for six weeks, or until late October when they were taken down, the leaves stripped from the stalks and pressed into hogsheads. By midcentury the hogshead had been standardized into a cask four feet high with a diameter of two and a half feet, weighing between a thousand and thirteen hundred pounds. The season finally ended in late November or early December when the hogsheads had been lifted aboard one of the tobacco ships that drifted up and down the streams of Tidewater country. The farmer had no control over the price he got for his crop. It depended on how British merchants had sized up the market. If he was lucky and the price high, he might have enough after he had paid off all his debts to buy from the ship's floating store a skillet or a length of calico for the wife, an ax or some fortified wine for himself.

The tobacco farmer now had three months to deal with things left undone—fences to build, new fields to open, firewood to cut, perhaps the addition of an outdoor kitchen to the house. Winter was a closed-in time in New England, where snow blocked travel until sleighs became common; in the Chesapeake conviviality rose to the surface, for people could travel easily over ground frozen but free of snow. This was the season, not the early summer for later generations, when young couples had the leisure to get married.

A New Breed of Man

It is hard to generalize about early American farmers. Judgments of them vary from Jefferson's idealization—"Those who labor in the earth are the chosen people of God, if ever He had a chosen people, whose breasts He has made His peculiar deposit for substantial and genuine virtue"—to the condemnation by a seventeenth-century Virginian who called them men who "sponge upon the blessings of a warm sun and fruitful soil, and almost grutch the pains of gathering in the bounties of the earth." This much, though, can be said with certainty: they differed within a few years of settlement from their English counterparts, not only in what they ate and what they raised, but in the way they lived. The semi-isolated farm not only affected social life and familial relations, but it forced men to do for themselves what they had once depended on village craftsmen to do for them. What Crèvecoeur had to say about the eighteenth-century American farmer holds for the man who came into being in the seventeenth century. "For most of us are skillful enough to use [tools] with some dexterity in mending and making whatever is wanted on the farm," he wrote. "Were we obliged to run to distant mechanics, who are half farmers themselves, many days would elapse, and we should always be behind hand in our work." The American farmer, says a later writer who could also have been describing his seventeenth-century predecessor, "makes almost every thing that he uses. Besides clearing the land, building houses, and making fences, he stocks his own plough, mends his wagon, makes his ox-yokes and harness, and learns to supply nearly all his wants from the forest. The tables, bedsteads, and seats in his house, are of his own rude workmanship." Out of the demands imposed by the farm on settlers came a new breed of man whose qualities are encapsulated in the American phrase "jack-of-all-trades."

4

THE HOUSE

Makeshift Beginnings

THE LAND imposed a rude existence on the earliest settlers. The first Englishmen pitched tents on the beaches, dug caves into hillsides, or took over abandoned Indian shelters. At Salem a man adapted the wigwam, adding a door at one end and a fireplace at the other. Here, in the first months he and his band "made [to] shift out the winter's cold by the fireside, . . . turning down many a drop of the bottle, and burning tobacco with all the ease they could, discoursing between one while and another of the great progress they would make after the summer's sun had changed the earth's white furred gown into a green mantle."

A common solution to the housing shortage up and down the coast was what later, on the Great Plains, came to be called the sod house. Noël Hume has shown it existed in early Virginia, but a Dutchman in 1650 also ascribed it to the first settlers of New Netherlands and New England. They, he said,

> dig a square pit in the ground, cellar fashion, six or seven feet deep, as long and as broad as they think proper, case the earth inside all

around the wall with timber, which they line with bark of trees or something else to prevent the caving in of the earth, floor this cellar with plank and wainscot it overhead for a ceiling, raise a roof of spars clear up and cover the spars with bark or green sods, so that they can live dry and warm in these houses with their entire families for two, three, or four years.

The first real houses were not much better than the original shelters, still little more than huts, still "decidedly substandard housing." These "ramshackle hovels," as Edmund Morgan has called them, persisted in the Chesapeake region and elsewhere well into the second half of the seventeenth century, "suggesting this was just a stopping place." A few of the better-off citizens eventually built with brick, "but everyone else still lived in the rotting wooden affairs that lay about the landscape like so many landlocked ships. A heavy storm would knock them down or fire devour them in an instant. But no matter—sift the ashes for nails and put up more—wood was cheap."

These huts were small, say twenty feet by twenty feet, and seldom rose over a story and a half high. A ladder or ladder-like stairway led to a loft, if there was one. Construction was simple: four posts or logs pounded into the ground with a siding of clapboard (riven planks five or six feet long lapped over each other when nailed to the posts), roofed with thatch or sod. The fireplace and chimney might be made of stone but more likely were built of logs plastered with clay. Light seeped in through slits of varying sizes, perhaps covered with glazed paper, waxed cloth, or pieces of animal horn scraped thin enough to be translucent. Shutters, a practical necessity then, not an ornament as now, helped keep winter winds out. Doorways were often small, forcing a visitor to stoop as he entered; he arrived headfirst, bent double, and if unfriendly was thus easy to disarm. What the early settler wanted, John Stilgoe remarks, "was an inward-focused house, a sure defense against human and animal enemies."

Mansions could be found in the port towns—a Boston merchant in 1660 owned a house with eleven rooms which with furnishings included was valued at over seven thousand pounds, then an enormous sum—but wretched dwellings persisted among the plain people to the end of the century. A visitor to Connecticut in 1704 came upon a house "supported with shores [corner posts] enclosed with clapboards laid on lengthways and so much asunder that light comes through everywhere; the doors tied on with a cord in the place of hinges; the floor the bare earth; no windows but such as the thin covering afforded, nor any furniture but a bed with a glass bottle hanging at the head on it, an earthen cup, a small pewter basin, a board with sticks to stand on instead of a table, and a block or two in the corner instead of chairs."

These early structures were dank, dark, and, worse, drafty. "We had a fire," said an overnight visitor to a clapboard house in New Jersey in 1679, but the house was "so wretchedly constructed that if you are not so close to the fire as almost to burn yourself, you cannot keep warm, for the wind blows through everywhere." The next night, only a few miles down the road, he stayed in a log cabin. He rhapsodized over it.

> The house, although not much larger than where we were the last night, was somewhat better and tighter, being made according to the Swedish mode, and as they usually build their houses here, which are block-houses, being nothing else than entire trees, split through the middle, or squared out of the rough, and placed in the form of a square, upon each other, as high as they wish to have the house; the ends of these timbers are let into each other, about a foot from the ends, half of one into half of the other. The whole structure is thus made without a nail or a spike. The ceiling and roof do not exhibit much finer work, except among the most careful people, who have the ceiling planked and a glass window. The doors are wide enough, but very low, so that you have to stoop in entering. These houses are quite tight and warm.

The log cabin was ideally suited to the inexperienced new-comer needing shelter in the wilderness. Even a city-bred man, once blisters had healed and he had learned to swing an ax, might construct one quickly and with ease. No carpenter could have built a snugger or more inexpensive house, yet few English settlers ventured to erect them. True, here and there some shed enough of their heritage to construct houses of squared logs "so tightly fitted inside that a knife blade could scarcely enter between them," but such venturesome Englishmen were rare. To judge by their houses, the settlers adjusted to the wilderness more slowly than the snail moved.

The Floor Plan

The first settlers sought to reproduce houses they had known at home. A man who came from a cold and windy part of England built his house low to the ground, four times as long as wide and without a second story; another from a more salubrious climate produced a boxlike affair with a loft or a second story. Those from areas where thatched roofs prevailed reproduced such roofs in America. Thus, the early types of houses varied from town to town, county to county, and even within those relatively small areas. Yet within a generation of settlement regional uniformity in housing had evolved. For Richard L. Bushman this evolution illustrates a cultural need for settlers from disparate backgrounds to express membership in a new group. "Adoption of a certain vernacular style represented a commitment to one's neighbors and to the norms that the local community valued," he writes. "The mixture of migrants from various regions within a single town intensified the need for a common culture to overarch . . . regional and religious peculiarities."

Practical considerations also helped to shape regional innovations. The contiguous lean-to added to the rear in both the North and South came early because it was a cheap and easy way to meet the needs of an expanding family. The substitution of shingles for thatched roofs reduced the risk of fire in the drier climate; also, their lightness compared to the slate roofing often found in England put less weight on the house frame. A cellar, generally unknown in England, became a common feature used to store food during the hot summers. In the North builders steepened the pitch of the roof to let snow slide off more easily. Also in the North the abundance of wood and the demands of colder winters led to a larger fireplace with the chimney centrally located to spread heat evenly through the house. In the hot and humid South, fireplaces were placed at the end of the house to "dissipate the heat generated in the summer by the constant need for cooking fires." Philadelphia, founded after the Great Fire of London, chose to build mainly of brick. The houses there were cramped structures that rose three stories high. "I say," a New England visitor wrote home, "give me a wooden one, that I may swing a cat around in."

The immediate and desperate need for shelter helped to speed the rise of standardized housing everywhere. Some twenty thousand people arrived in Massachusetts Bay within a decade. In 1682 alone two thousand settlers flooded into the Delaware Valley and another two thousand came the next year. Each of these migrants knew the kind of house he wanted—one like the house he had just left—but few knew how to build one. Those from cities and port towns, even those from villages, had lived in dwellings that had been passed down from one generation to the next. They had no experience constructing a house from the ground up. More often than not they had to draw on the skill of an itinerant master builder or carpenter. The well-to-do might tell him exactly the sort of house they wanted, but plain people who needed roofs over their heads quickly had to accept the fixed floor plan he offered.

He arrived on the scene with a blueprint in his head, a two-foot folding rule in his pocket, and only an experienced eye to judge whether beams were plumb and level. (The spirit level would not be invented until the 1660s.) The tools he carried had changed little since the days of the Roman Empire—crosscut and rip saws, hammers, chisels, mallets, augers, gimlets, planes, hatchets and axes. He favored huge timbers for the frame—a ton or more of wood went into even a small house—because tradition told him such were needed to support the structure. He used wooden pegs to hold everything together because nails were expensive. The pegs, carved from hardwood, were, after long drying to prevent shrinking, pounded into beams with the ends sticking out; at the first sign of a wobbling rafter they were pounded in further.

When a site had been chosen he passed out directions—the uprights must be of a certain thickness and length, the rafters of another size, the clapboards of a particular shape. He then moved on to another site, returning when his orders had been carried out to supervise the raising of the house. In time, when a settler needed more space and he had acquired some skill with ax and saw, the house might take on an individual shape that suited him and his family's needs, but the basic floor plan remained that of the master builder.

Despite local and regional variations a few generalizations can be made about these early floor plans. There were no rooms with assigned functions, no bedroom, as such, no dining room, no bathroom. (Indeed, down to the end of the seventeenth century few houses had even a chamber pot, or "looking glass," as it was called. Members of the family, regardless of age or sex or the weather, relieved themselves in the privy outside.) The loft was for sleeping but also served as storage space. There were no closets; the few garments were packed in chests or hung from pegs scattered about the house.

In the beginning the ground floor was given over to the "hall," as it was called, although a small "inner room" might be set apart for the husband and wife's privacy. As a rule, however, the seventeenth-century house had no room for privacy. If one wanted to be alone, to sulk, to lose one's temper, there was no place to go but outside. The hall was not just a component in

THOMAS YARDLEY   THOMAS STACKHOUSE   HENRY PAXSON

Examples of ear markings. Cattle rustling was a common offense in early America. Farmers tried to limit their losses by clipping the ears of their beasts, registering the pattern they chose with local authorities, much as ranch brands would be in a later period. *(Pennsylvania Historical and Museum Commission)*

An early plow made of wood and iron. *(Smithsonian Institution)*

A seventeenth-century New England fireplace. *(Metropolitan Museum of Art, New York)*

A bellows was defined as "an Instrument invented to make wind and is used to blow up fires for their more speedy Kindling." The elaborate one pictured here was made in England in 1696. Those found in the average person's house were usually homemade and unadorned. *(Museum of Fine Arts, Boston)*

This skillet was made in England probably in the latter part of the seventeenth century. The long handle let the housewife remove it from the fire without burning herself. *(Colonial Williamsburg Foundation)*

A goblet of this size was rare even in late seventeenth-century America, when this one was made. It was probably used for celebratory or ceremonial occasions when each guest took a sip from it as it was passed about the assembly. *(Museum of Fine Arts, Boston)*

According to one seventeenth-century definition, "a chafing dish is a kind of round iron, made hollow like a basin, set on feet, either three or four, with an handle to move it from place to place; its office is to hold hot coals of fire in, and to set dish-meats thereupon, to keep them warm till the time of serving them up to the table, or to heat a cold dish of meat, on the table." This one was made in either England or Holland sometime after 1680. *(Colonial Williamsburg Foundation)*

The tines of these forks are of steel, the handles of horn. They were made in England during the latter half of the seventeenth century. They were used to hold down meat as it was cut with a knife and not to convey food to the mouth. The act of lifting food to the mouth with a fork came only when the three-tined fork arrived sometime around 1690. *(Colonial Williamsburg Foundation)*

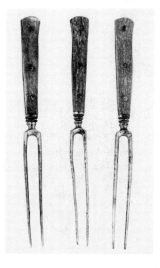

On the other side of this tankard showing an engraved portrait of William of Orange, king of England from 1689 to 1702, are etched a rose, a unicorn, and a thistle, all symbols of the monarchy. A tankard as elaborate as this has been called the aristocrat of drinking vessels in seventeenth-century England and America. *(Colonial Williamsburg Foundation)*

This portrait of Alice Mason, age two in 1670, by an unknown artist, shows how children were considered to be miniature adults. *(U.S. Department of the Interior)*

"The squareness of the toe is accentuated by a slight overhang of the tip, and the thick sole is a single piece of leather that extends up to the front of the heel and from the heel lift," Linda Wesselman writes. "The tabs of the shoe were crossed at the top of the high tongue and were secured by a removable buckle." This shoe was made either in England or New England around 1650. *(Museum of Fine Arts, Boston)*

Such high-crowned beaver hats were worn by men and women of fashion in England from the early seventeenth century on. The Massachusetts General Court in 1634 limited the right to wear them to those who held property worth two hundred pounds or more, a large sum at the time. This particular hat is supposed to have arrived in America aboard the *Mayflower*. *(Pilgrim Society, Plymouth, Mass.)*

These fringed gloves, which date back at least to 1645, were owned by Governor John Leverett of Massachusetts. They were worn only on ceremonial occasions. Gold and silver threads are woven through the fringed cuffs. *(Essex Institute, Salem, Mass.)*

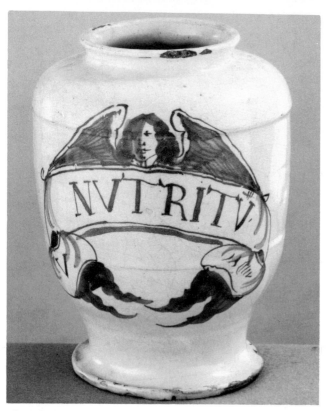

This glazed apothecary pot was probably made in London sometime around 1670. *(Colonial Williamsburg Foundation)*

These three visible lancet blades, and one concealed in the brass case, were made of steel. The lancet was a standard item in the medicine bag of seventeenth-century American physicians. *(Colonial Williamsburg Foundation)*

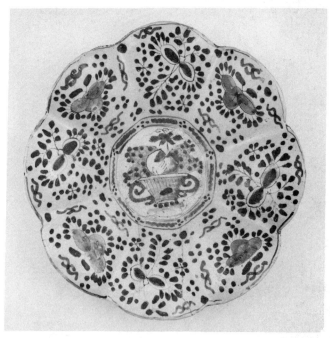

This elaborately-shaped, lobed dish, colored in blue, came from Holland sometime between 1660 and 1700. It could be used as a serving dish but more often, accompanied by a ewer filled with scented water, was used by diners to rinse their hands after a meal. *(Essex Institute, Salem, Mass.)*

This bronze and iron kettle, made in England around 1650, is somewhat unusual in that it has legs that allow it to be placed directly in the fire, but also a handle so that it can hang above the flames. *(Colonial Williamsburg Foundation)*

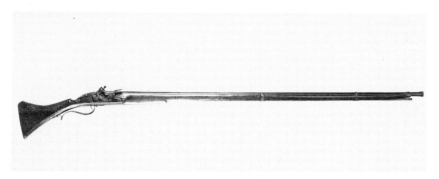

This fowling piece was made in England and carried to Connecticut in 1640. It is one of the earliest among the few surviving weapons connected with early New England. Note especially the graceful spoon-shaped trigger guard. *(Smithsonian Institution)*

This heavy oxhide coat was made in England sometime in the mid-1640s and owned by Governor George Leverett of Massachusetts Bay. As originally designed it bore clasps of either gold or silver, and a belt or buckle to hold a sword. Such coats were originally worn beneath armor, but when it became apparent that its thickness, a quarter of an inch, blunted bullets and arrows, it was worn without armor. It has been noted that punctures and bloodstains on the coat's arms and skirts reveal that Leverett must have been wounded while wearing it. *(Massachusetts Historical Society, Boston)*

the house, like the modern living room, but the spot where life within was truly lived. Here meals were cooked and eaten, here the family prayed, and here by the flickering light of the fireplace members carried on whatever work could be performed inside. The fireplace dominated the room.

As the family and its possessions expanded, so too did the house. One of the first additions carried cooking and the disarray that went with it out of the hall to what in some areas came to be called the "keeping room." The hall now became the "best room," where guests could be entertained. Next might come the lean-to at the rear, which in some houses became the kitchen, in others a storage place for tools and dairy equipment. To keep the heat from the cooking fire out of the house in summer, the Chesapeake came to favor a kitchen detached from the house. Later, as the family prospered, the inner room could be transformed into the parlor, where the family's valuables—silver, glassware, and books—might be displayed. It could be used to give privacy to courtships, and often children were born in the parlor, sometimes called the "borning room." The room, however, had little to do with the family's everyday life. That continued to center in the hall.

A seventeenth-century hall reassembled in a museum today, stripped of its inhabitants, of the smoke and smell and noise of daily living, looks warm and comfortable, a tranquil spot. It may have seemed otherwise—cramped, dirty, oppressively close— to those who lived in it. Turn down the museum lights and view the room by a candle or two; it becomes a gloomy place. But this again imposes a modern judgment. People of the seventeenth century may not have minded being closed off from a view of trees and sky; it may have pleased them to shut the outdoors out. "To them," John Demos has said, "Nature was no long-lost love, to be courted and admired at every opportunity. To them, indeed, she frequently presented herself in the guise of antagonist, and they saw no reason to try and make place for her in their home."

The Fireplace

Life withindoors centered around the fireplace. In any modern reconstruction of the interior of a supposedly typical colonial hall the fireplace presents a muddle of heavy wrought ironware. Andirons support the logs. A lug pole with a variety of hooks, chains, and trammels hanging from it stretches across the mouth. Tools for handling the fire—a shovel to remove ashes, tongs to shift logs, a pair of bellows to fan embers alive—are piled at one edge of the hearth, and around the rim are heaps of cooking equipment—ladles, saucepans, skillets, pots, cauldrons, and the like. While the cookware is ponderous and must have tested a woman's strength, the variety and abundance suggest a well-appointed kitchen. The depiction is misleading. Many, perhaps most, colonial houses deep into the century were not so amply equipped. Wills that have survived often give a starker picture. One farmer, for instance, lists only "one kettle pot and pot hooks, one old kettle" as cookware, and another "an iron kettle, old iron pot and pot hooks . . . a ladle . . . an iron hook to hang a pot on."

Wood was plentiful and winters, even in the Chesapeake region, colder than those known in England. For these reasons, a colonial fireplace was at least twice the size of an English yeoman's, so large, indeed, that the word *fireplace* is misleading; "a place of fires" would put it better. The central fire warmed the house. Embers raked to one side gave a bed of glowing coals to boil a kettle. At the other side another small fire might be heating the bakeoven. If there was no oven, a pie or loaf of bread, covered with an iron pot, could sit to bake on a cleared space of the hot hearthstone. If after supper the wife needed light to spin by or the husband to whittle, say, new pegs or new teeth for a wooden rake or hay fork, the family kindled a fire of thin, dry wood, which gave a bright clear flame as it crackled away.

A house with a single fireplace burned between fifteen and twenty cords of wood a year (a cord measures four by four by eight feet), or something between three and four fifths of an acre of standing timber. A farmer spent a good deal of his time collecting wood for his fire, hauling it to the house, and chopping it into lengths that would fit the fireplace. The longer he lived on his plot the farther he had to go for his fuel.

No day passed when the fireplace went unused. As a result, soot accumulated quickly in the chimney. This could be hazardous when firs were the principal source for fuel, for they left behind a thick, tarry, highly flammable coating. Brooms were used to clean short chimneys. For taller ones it was not uncommon to drop a chicken or two down the chimney; their frantic wing-beating did a good cleaning job quickly.

Furnishings

As the distance between rich and poor widened toward the end of the seventeenth century, those at the top turned to Europe to furnish their houses. When Virginia's well-to-do William Byrd, Sr., began to build a mansion in 1690, he sent to Rotterdam for bedsteads, curtains, tables, and upholstered chairs. Fragile porcelain replaced pewter on his dining table. But the furnishings of Byrd's house were no more typical of the time than those of a Newport mansion in the Gilded Age.

The average seventeenth-century farmhouse might look cluttered, yet was sparsely furnished by modern standards. In the Chesapeake more than half the households contained personal belongings worth less than sixty pounds. About a third of the families there had chairs or benches but only one house in seven owned both. If the husband were adept at carpentry, the hall might hold a corner cupboard to store eating utensils and other small items. Beds for many years were a rarity. A bedroll or "shake-down" that could be rolled up during the day was common at least during the early years of settlement. The family ate from a long board or pair of boards nailed together, which stood on trestles close to the fireplace. No one called it a dining table. It was, instead, the board table, and the cloth that covered it, if the family had one, the board cloth. To sit "at the board" was to eat, and a hired hand expected both "room and board" as part of his pay. In the beginning, when smooth boards were hard to come by, the top of a packing case might be used; one such tabletop still exists, with the name and address of the Boston family to whom it was sent in 1638 on its underside. The family sat on benches, stools, or chests pushed up to the board. Chairs were not then common. If the family had one it was reserved for the head of the house—thus the word *chairman*.

The table setting was simple. In the center lay the salt cellar. Adults and guests sat "above the salt," children and servants below. Most of the tableware was unbreakable and until a family could afford pewter more likely than not made of wood. There were no individual settings. Diners paired up, sharing a common trencher—a wooden tray about ten inches square and depressed in the center like a modern soup bowl. Trencher mates drank from shared wooden or leather noggins. Spoons were the essential utensil at the table. Knives, if they turned up, were pointed and used to spear food from the common serving dish. Forks did not appear until the eighteenth century. There were those who held that forks were "a diabolical luxury," and that "God would not have given us fingers if He had wished us to use such an instrument." The arrival of the fork in England led to a change in the table knife; the pointed end became curved. Americans imported their knives and thus got the new version before they got the fork. They now used the spoon, with the curved end held down, to anchor food while cutting it with the knife, reversing the spoon to carry the food from plate to mouth. When the fork finally arrived, they used it as they had the spoon. "Which is precisely the way we use it today," James Deetz has pointed out. "This distinctive way of using the knife, fork, and spoon came into existence during the late seventeenth and early eighteenth centuries, and thus is one more American idiosyncrasy arising from isolation during that period."

Beyond the board table and scattered along the walls of the hall before additions to the house were made, the family scattered items used with some regularity—seasonal clothing and tools like saws, guns, hoes, axes, possibly a spinning wheel or a loom. If the family had prospered, the hall or the inner room might hold a bedstead or two. To save space, a trundle bed, for infants, could be pulled out from under the "parent bed" at night and tucked beneath it during the day. Another way to save space was to hinge a bedstead to the wall, much like a Pullman berth of later centuries; it could be raised out of the way come dawn. The most common bedstead mattress was a bag stuffed with rags, corn husks, possibly bits of wool or other soft material that lay ready at hand. The loft and the lean-to, if the family had them, doubled as sleeping and storage space, but they seldom held beds. Often the floor of the loft lay loose on the joists so that the boards could be removed when items like barrels, too bulky to negotiate the steep stairs, needed to be raised or lowered.

Within this small, crowded space, day in and day out, lived a family that might number up to a dozen members, varying in age from a year or less up to seventy or more years. Artifacts that have survived from seventeenth-century America have been passed down from those who prospered. They bequeathed an impression of a comfortable if not sumptuous way of life. The everyday life of the plain people of the time shared little in this easy existence. The rude upbringing of Abraham Lincoln nearly two centuries later on a frontier nearly a thousand miles inland from the Atlantic differed little from what the early settlers endured in the seventeenth century.

5

THE HOME

Some Assumptions and Generalizations

A NUMBER of years ago John Demos, in a study of Bristol, Rhode Island, in colonial times, came up with conclusions about family life in early America that contravened ideas handed down from the past. Among the inherited assumptions and his opinions about them were the following:

> The colonial family was "extended" rather than "nuclear." *False.*
> Children in a colonial family were numerous. *True with qualifications.*
> The normal age of marriage was early. *False.*

Demos's conclusions have held up well enough over the years to be broadened from Bristol to include all New England; they apply equally well to the Middle Colonies in the latter part of the seventeenth century.

The house in New England and elsewhere shaped the home. Even in an age that put no premium on privacy, an extended family that included servants, apprentices, and other non-kinfolk could not survive in a house that measured twenty feet by twenty feet and rose only a story and a half. The addition of

another room or a lean-to still gave only enough space for a
nuclear family—father, mother, and children. The number of
children in a family was high—Sir William Phips was one of
twenty-six, Benjamin Franklin one of seventeen, but the average hovered between seven and ten. However, the number in
the home seldom exceeded three or four. Early death took
some from the scene, others were apprenticed out, and those
who married left promptly. Given the myths about early marriages, they married late—mid-twenties for the men, early
twenties for the women—but soon enough to rear their own
passel of offspring. Over the years the number within a typical
family seldom went beyond six or seven.

Demos's study draws further conclusions about old assumptions.

The mortality rate for infants and mothers in childbirth was high.
Much exaggerated.
Life expectancy was low. *False.*
Men and women were married two or more times, owing to the
death of first spouse. *Much exaggerated.*

These judgments, too, have held up well over the years. In
colonial New England every fifth woman died from causes tied
to childbirth, a figure high by modern standards but low given
assumptions about the period; infant mortality was one out of
ten. It was not uncommon for parents to live out their biblical
allotment of threescore and ten years. Given the long life of
married couples, remarriage was, as Demos concludes, "much
exaggerated." But when Demos's conclusions are expanded beyond the borders of New England they begin to disintegrate. In
the South life expectancy well into the seventeenth century was
low for everyone. Women died often in childbirth and their
offspring with them. Of the children who survived, to judge by
the records of one county in Virginia, nearly a third lost one
parent by the age of nine, another quarter lost both by the
age of thirteen, and fewer than a third had both alive at the

age of eighteen. Grandparents were all but nonexistent. The early death of a spouse led to remarriage, often more than once.

Recent scholarship has shown that no generalization seems to hold up. "On the face of it," Daniel Blake Smith has said, "the historiography of the early American family defies any all-embracing interpretation." Several factors shaped the American family. First, the English background, for at the time of settlement, England "was the scene of considerable disagreement about the proper way to raise children." Ethnic and religious factors also entered. The Dutch in New York, the Germans and Swedes in Pennsylvania brought their own conceptions of what a family should be. Quakers in the Delaware Valley and Congregationalists in New England seem to have demanded tight-knit families dominated by a patriarch. Finally, environment entered in. "In the South," the Rutmans have observed, "were comparatively unstable families, where early parental death, a profusion of orphans, the frailty of overarching religious values made for a 'modern-like' family."

Still, the historian cannot resist generalizations. Here are several, again drawn from Demos, that would seem to hold up for the family wherever found in early America. It was

a business
a vocational institute
a house of correction
a church
a welfare institution

Regardless of when or where the immigrants settled, the family formed a web that continued to make sense of Donne's view that no man was an island. Every member of the family from the age of three or so onward had a role to play; the family's welfare to an extent depended on how he or she played it. Crops had to be planted, tended, harvested. Cows had to be milked, hogs slaughtered and salted down. If a child learned to read, someone in the family taught him. The family, not just the father and mother, shaped deportment. Religion, especially among isolated families, began and ended with morning and evening prayers. Kinfolk who could not care for themselves—the spinster, who sat by the fire spinning, the senile or otherwise disabled relative—had somehow to be fitted into the snug but small house.

The Clan

" 'Tis all in peeces, all coharence gone," John Donne remarked early in the seventeenth century. He spoke of the new cosmology that men like Kepler were creating, but he could as well have been thinking of the pattern of daily life that had been shattered in America, where the village had ceased to be central to most men's lives and the home had seemingly become an isolated unit in the wilderness. Europeans had failed to see, and most historians along with them, that with the waning of village life the colonists did not lose their sense of community. They transferred it to the family and in so doing gave a new meaning to an old word. Forget catch phrases like "nuclear family" and "extended family," which sociologists and, alas, many colonial historians favor; they only obscure what happened. The family came now to embrace all blood relations, or kinfolk, in the neighborhood. (As previously remarked, the word *neighborhood* also took on new, broader meaning to include an area reachable by horseback or canoe within a day, say, a radius of fifty miles.)

For some reason *clan*—a community of kinfolk—never caught on in America, which is unfortunate because it clarifies what the word *family* beclouds—a unique way to keep alive a sense of community. The clan came to do what the village had done in England. It provided for its own—the orphans, the ill, the indigent—much as the village had, often in a more personal way. The way in which the Chesapeake evolved "was not as an area of isolated plantations and individuals but as a mosaic of close-knit neighborhoods and kinship groups," the Rutmans have written. "The home was not an isolated castle but a neighborhood focal point. . . . The typical family was not the neat nuclear one of mother-father-children but a mixed affair of parents, stepparents, guardians, natural children, stepchildren, and wards."

"It could hardly be otherwise," they go on, "given the prevalance of illness, the frequency of early death, and the necessity of caring for the sick and orphaned; and it can be argued that in the Chesapeake region the form and strength of the social bonds were direct corollaries of the fragility of life." But what the Rutmans say of the Chesapeake is relevant to other parts of early America. In East Guilford, Connecticut, a town that lacked a strong village core, almost 40 percent of the families were related to each other. Here, as in the South, duties an English village performed the clan carried out. From the evidence that survives, the same holds true throughout the Middle Colonies. Families differed one from another, according to ethnic and religious backgrounds and the effects of environment, but the concept of the clan seems to have been pervasive. A call for help from a faraway relative was answered; the clan would respond with obloquy if it were not. Members of the clan could hate one another, but when a senile elder, an orphan, a decrepit old lady called for care, the matter was somehow solved. The webs were as tight as they had been in Europe, only they were different webs. But none forgot that the strength of the clan depended on the sturdiness of the home within that clan.

Women

There is a famous quotation from the journal of John Winthrop often used to encapsulate the male attitude toward women in early America. A young woman had lost "her understanding and reason" because she had given "herself wholly to reading and writing, and written many books." If she had kept her place, Winthrop said, "if she had attended to household affairs, and such things as belong to women, and not gone out of her way and calling to meddle in such things as are proper for men, whose minds are stronger, etc., she had kept her wits, and might have improved them usefully and honorably in the place God had set her."

Winthrop's observations perpetuate the views of a seventeenth-century upper-class English gentleman who is unaware of the changes that had affected woman's role in the everyday life of early America. She still performed a number of fixed duties as in England—prepared meals, milked cows, washed clothes, tended to the kitchen garden and the beehives if the family had them. But her role was no longer limited to household chores. In a land with a chronic shortage of labor she now became the husband's partner in the fields, especially at planting time and again during the harvest season. Deference to the man still remained, yet what has been said of the New England woman applies generally to all in early America—"this does not seem to have been a society characterized by a really pervasive, an operational norm, of male dominance."

Generalizations are no easier to devise about the everyday life of colonial women than about the colonial family. Two case studies—one for Maryland, the other for Salem, Massachusetts —help to illuminate two of probably several divergent patterns that developed over time in different environments.

A study of the seventeenth-century Maryland planter's wife, by Lois Green Carr and Lorena S. Walsh, embodies two stories, one of the immigrant woman who arrived during the first half of the century, the other of her native-born daughter. Nearly all the early incoming women came as indentured servants. The typical woman was single, between eighteen and twenty-five years old, and no doubt in search of a husband. First, however, she was obliged to serve out her indenture, and since the law forbade a servant to marry until she had completed her contract, that meant four or five years must pass before she could get a husband. They were devastating years. Exposure to malaria left her susceptible to more deadly diseases. The physical work was harder than anything she had known in England. If she served a small planter, she had, in addition to household chores, the fields to tend. She was easily exploited and degraded, for on an isolated farm there were few effective checks to the authority of the planter or his ofttimes shrewish wife. If the woman bore a bastard child, as some 20 percent did, she paid heavily for the transgression—physical punishment, months added to her service for time lost to the planter, and, worst of all, the possibility of having her child bound out to another family. Only if the father of the child bought up her contract could she escape into marriage, but all too often the father was a fellow bonded servant.

If the woman lived through her service, a quick marriage was inevitable in a land where men outnumbered women seven to one. "Comely or homely, strong or weak, any young woman was too valuable to be overlooked, and most could find a man with prospects." But she could be choosy only up to a point, for about a third of the women were pregnant at the time of marriage, about twice the rate in England at the time. Marriage did not necessarily mean that life improved measurably. As a commodity the woman was an object that could not be treated brutally or tyrannically. If intelligent, thrifty, and hardy, she became more than a helpmeet, as were English wives; she became a partner, sharing in her husband's efforts to scrabble a living from the wilderness. But her daily grind was grueling as ever. Now she had a home to run, children to rear, and still the hoe in hand when the season and the fields called for it. The death rate remained high for husband and wife, but slightly higher for her, as, weakened by malaria, she often failed to survive childbirth. Both, however, shared the specter of an early death. Chances were only one in three that they would live out ten years of married life together. Statistics were no better for their children. Half the offspring would not reach maturity. A survey of 105 Maryland families between 1660 and 1680 produced only twelve parents who left more than three children behind.

The immigrant woman who survived her childbearing years, say, to the age of forty-five, usually outlived her husband. The common sharing that early farm life demanded led the husband to trust his wife, and generosity usually prevailed in his will. More often than not he gave to her more than the third of his land the law required. "On the whole," Carr and Walsh remark, a survey of extant wills attests to "the husband's overriding concern for the welfare of his widow and to his confidence in her management, regardless of the certainty of her remarriage. Evidently, in the politics of family life women enjoyed great respect." As inevitably as the once-indentured woman married when free, she remarried when her husband died, especially if she had no son old enough to manage the farm. But now she could be choosy and more demanding. Into the marriage she brought property and possibly children who could work the land. She also brought the experience of a previous partnership and an authority that her English counterparts had never shared. She was not someone who could be pushed around easily. Legally she remained inferior to her husband, and she could not participate openly in public affairs, but within the family she had a very strong voice.

Life differed considerably for her native-born daughter. Seldom did she have to endure servitude outside the home. This freed her to marry younger, and the mean age for marriage of Maryland women born in the second half of the century dropped to sixteen and a half years. However, one thing remained constant: approximately 20 percent of the women were pregnant before they married. For reasons not entirely clear, life expectancy improved in the latter part of the century, with the result that marriages lasted longer and more children reached maturity. As the family grew and sons could now do what she had once done in the fields, she became more domestic. The home now became her domain, and with the shift in roles she slowly lost some of the power she had once held within the family.

A study of Salem between 1636 and 1683 by C. Dallett Hemphill suggests something similar happened there, despite a radically different environment. There families were stable. Men and women generally lived long lives, infant mortality was low, and most children lived to maturity. And yet there, as in Maryland, the woman during the early part of the century shared in all sides of her husband's life on the farm. She worked the land with him, tended livestock, even joined in branding the steers. The village court records, Hemphill remarks, "reinforce notions of partnership and mutual obligation in marriage that modify the conception of patriarchal deference." However, over the years Salem changed from a farming village into a mercantile town, and as it changed male and female roles diverged. "As husbands became gunsmiths, coopers, cutters, or schoolmasters, and thus less dependent on agriculture for subsistence, their wives' share in familial economic production fell off." She could no longer share in her man's daily routine. By the end of the century the woman in Salem, as in Maryland, had been forced back into her traditional role. The home, not the farm, once again became her domain.

Children

John Locke held that the children of plain people should begin useful work at the age of three. The dictum of a philosopher, and a bachelor at that, should not be taken as the rule that guided early American parents. There is reason to think that Dr. Spock would find much to approve in the way colonial children were reared. In most homes the upbringing was strict and children were taught early about the horrible punishments that awaited in Hell for those who flouted parental authority, but it is too often forgotten that such strictness was laced with affection. A New England farmer who went to town to barter several bushels of rye returned home with items needed in the house and also a whistle and a doll. "When I was a child," one man recalled, "I was nurtured and tutored with such fatherly care and motherly affection as my parents at that time were endued with." Another man recalled his mother's strict hand but also the "great love" she gave him.

The quality of a colonial childhood varied, as always, with the character of the parents as well as their religious and ethnic backgrounds. Congregationalists, Presbyterians, and Quakers were stricter, Anglicans and Dutch Lutherans more easygoing with their children. Regardless of their religious ties, it is also too often forgotten that many, if not most, parents knew how hard life could be and looked upon childhood as a time to be enjoyed as much as possible. Too much has been made of the fire-and-brimstone sermons that aimed to break children's rebellious spirits. Parents then as now tended to be more tolerant than they liked to admit. Colonial children were initiated into the adult world early but not in a hasty or harsh manner. From the age of three or so they were given chores, partly for discipline but also to keep them from underfoot. Much of a child's day passed with little supervision; parents and older siblings were too busy to mind what they did. They trusted the children early with responsibilities that would horrify a modern parent. John Adams was given a gun when only eight, just old enough to lift it, and alone, under no watchful adult eye, he spent hours, day after day, in the marshes bringing down birds, or trying to.

The colonial child moved toward adulthood in a fairly straight line, with no pause for the miseries of adolescence. That phase, except in its physical manifestations, did not exist then, and the word itself did not achieve general use until the twentieth century. In the seventeenth century, as opposed to later periods, "the environmental setting was much simpler—and the process of growth inherently less difficult," John Demos remarks. "Development toward full maturity could be accomplished in a gradual, piecemeal, and largely automatic fashion. There were few substantial choices to be made; the boy's own father, or the girl's own mother, provided relatively clear models for the formation of a meaningful 'identity.' Here was no 'awkward age' —but the steady lengthening of a young person's shadow." Nor was there a profound "generation gap." The father passed on to the son the way he had been taught to clear the ground or build a house and the son in turn passed it on to his son. Outwardly there was little that changed in the world from one generation to the next. Fads occasionally turned up, as in Boston in the 1650s when a shocked citizenry saw young men with a "lust for long hair" worn "like woman's hair," but such aberrations rocked a stable world only momentarily.

The road to adulthood was simpler but not necessarily more tranquil than in later centuries. Often at an early age a child might be ripped from his family and apprenticed out to another one. Regardless of the reason—to learn a craft, to clear space in the small house for another child coming along, possibly to receive a stricter discipline than the parents felt able to apply —the experience must often have been traumatic. Childhood in the South could be harrowing during more than half of the seventeenth century when death rates were high and youths were likely to lose at least one parent and possibly two before reaching maturity. If lucky, they might find themselves embedded in a warm, protective "network of relatives and quasi-relatives" who cared for them as if they were their own; if unlucky, they might be separated from brothers and sisters, cheated out of their inheritances, and otherwise exploited. The orphan's court sought to protect them, but not always with success.

The education of the century's children was a haphazard affair, something that delighted a royal appointee like Governor William Berkeley. When asked by the Crown in 1671 about education in his colony, he replied: "I thank God, *there are no free schools* nor *printing* [in Virginia] and I hope we shall not have these hundred years; for *learning* has brought disobedience, and heresy, and sects into the world, and *printing* has divulged them, and libels against the best government. God keep us from both!"

Sometimes a minority view is made to reflect the majority. Berkeley spoke for himself, not the settlers of early America, most of whom came with respect for education. Most emerged from a Protestant nation which held that the ability to read God's word directly from the Bible (indirectly from the Book of Common Prayer) was essential to a godly life. Grammar schools, free for the poor, proliferated in seventeenth-century England, and an eagerness to recreate them in America existed everywhere. A Virginia planter in 1635 deeded two hundred acres of land and the income from eight milk cows to establish a charity school. Massachusetts Bay twice, in 1641 and 1647, tried to force its towns to erect and subsidize schools for all. The Dutch in New York tied church and education so tightly together that they created what came to be called the parochial school. William Penn's Frame of Government in 1681 called for children throughout his colony to be given a grasp of the three Rs.

Not much happened. Plymouth Colony had no school until the 1670s, a half century after settlement. Schools were expensive in all ways: schoolhouses had to be built and maintained, schoolmasters paid, and the children who attended were diverted from what they did on the farm. A youngster who arrived in New England in 1635 "with a little keeping at school" spent the next seven years helping his family clear the ground, then, when less needed on the farm, was apprenticed to his brother, a craftsman. With a wilderness to transform into living space, the people had little time to give over to reading and writing. Settlers of New England, who especially respected

learning, were not, one man said, "a people who counted ignorance the mother of devotion," yet the great part of them were
"wholly devoted to the plow." How, he asked, as settlers everywhere must have asked, were they to make the plow and learning "go on together"? Answer: "As yet they know not how."

In some way lost to the present they made the plow and
learning go together. The achievement evokes respect. There
were few books and no newspapers for these farmers until the
end of the century, yet among them learning persisted. Education for the plain people, north and south, centered in the
family. What they thought called for, what they wanted, came
about. Since women were generally restricted from learning—
it did, of course, lead, as John Winthrop said, to insanity—the
drive within families must have come from the father. The
drive, clearly, was utilitarian. A son must learn to add to make
clear at the end of the year where a family stood with the
shipmaster of a tobacco ship or a port-town merchant. A son
must learn to read and write if he wants to have a hand in
running public affairs. Regardless of the reasons, the achieve-
ments of the seventeenth-century settlers, given their largely
isolated lives, seems remarkable. The literacy level among male
youngsters who survived into adulthood in New England is not
especially impressive, given the high number of educated gentlemen who emigrated into the region. It was 60 percent in
1660, but rose only to 69 percent at the end of the century. The
statistics for the Chesapeake are more impressive, given the
background of the first settlers. It rose from 46 percent in the
1640s to 62 percent at the end of the century. All these figures
are debatable, for they are based on white male adults who
could sign their wills. Nonetheless, they are, one likes to think,
remarkable for people who somehow found the drive, energy,
and determination to learn to write, if not read, in a wilderness.

Addendum

The statement that early Americans could "write, if not read,"
has been questioned by one reader. It is, he writes, "faithful to
what we can verify empirically, but probably wrong in emphasis. All of the literature on early modern literacy seems to suggest that *many* more could read than write, that in some places,
reading was near-universal for males and not less for females,
while writing skills were less frequent."

6

HEALTH

A Physical Checkup

THE FIRST thing that struck every visitor to early America was the bad teeth of the people, especially of the women. "The women are pitifully tooth-shaken," John Josselyn reported; "whether through the coldness of the climate, or by sweetmeats, of which they have a score, I am not able to affirm." (Benjamin Franklin, a century later, attributed the affliction to eating frozen apples and hot soup.) Josselyn, with his usual certainty, had a cure: "brimstone and gunpowder compounded with butter; rub the mandible with it, the outside being first warmed."

Bad teeth excepted, the quality of health in America varied from region to region and from locality to locality through the seventeenth century, but overall it was far better in the North than in the South. During the first half of the century, the mortality rate ran as high as 80 percent in the Chesapeake. Typhoid and dysentery appear to have been the major killers, possibly propagated by polluted wells. Edmund Morgan thinks that health in the region improved with the appearance of orchards; the settlers not only had fresh fruit to supplement their diets but cider to drink in place of water. Regardless of the reason, the Chesapeake region after 1650 apparently became more "wholesome, healthy, and fruitful" than it had been, but still not as healthy as New England. Darrett and Anita Rutman attribute the continuing "fragility of life in the early Chesapeake" to the arrival of a virulent strain of malaria. It rarely killed victims, but "the great debilitator" left them enervated and susceptible to other diseases. It probably accounts for the high death rate of Chesapeake women in childbirth, and it may well have affected the life span of the entire population. According to the Rutmans, a young male adult from Andover, Massachusetts, who had reached the age of twenty could expect to live forty-five years longer, and a female from the same town could generally count on forty-two more years. A person of the same age from Middlesex County, Virginia, however, had an additional life expectancy of only twenty-nine years if male and twenty years if female. Andover was a virtual health resort compared to Middlesex County. There only one child in five died before the age of twenty. Half the females and three fifths of the males lived to be fifty. Three men in ten and almost as many women survived to seventy.

England in the seventeenth century, Carl Bridenbaugh has said, was "a sickly nation of country people. Ill-housed, seldom warm, generally under-nourished, they offered little resistance to afflictions and disease." New Englanders relatively speaking were paragons of health, and the people of the Chesapeake region were no worse and possibly slightly better off than their brethren back home, at least after 1650. Famines were still common in England and on the Continent—France suffered eleven national famines and scores of local ones during the seventeenth century—but a rarity in America. The settlers were generally better nourished and, except where malaria was endemic, abler to resist disease when it struck. The absence of large concentrations of population reduced the severity of epidemics when they came. The medical care for the people was as good if not better than in England. So much has been made of "the tragic role played by sickness and disease" in early America that it is well to remember that the health of the settlers during the latter half of the century was really not so bad.

What They Ate

Virtually every settlement went through a "starving time." The reasons were many. First-comers usually arrived too weak to hunt, exhausted from the trip over. But even those with energy to explore the forests were handicapped; few were familiar with guns, the prerogative of gentlemen back home. In time the settlers learned how to draw their food from the water, the sky, and the forest, and it was a rare household by the end of the century that could not serve up a hardy meal for an unexpected visitor. Hosts, as always, tended to show off, as the menu recorded by a visitor to New York suggests.

> We had for supper a roasted haunch of venison . . . which weighed thirty pounds. The meat was exceedingly tender and good and also quite fat. It had a slight spice flavor. We were also served with wild turkey, which was also fat and of a good flavor; and a wild goose, but that was rather dry. Everything we had was the natural production of the country.

Later he was persuaded to sample the meat of a raccoon, "a wild animal somewhat larger than a cat," and native to America. "It was very fat and of a good flavor, almost like a pig."

Meals were leaner in winter, but over the year settlers did not as a rule want for food. They took from the water all they could catch except salmon, which for reasons unknown they did not like, and shad, which they "profoundly despised." The Dutch especially relished oysters, which one traveler described as "large and full, some of them not less than a foot long." Summer saw meals laced with huckleberries, blackberries, and blueberries (also called "skycolored" berries). Wild strawberries matured in June. "They usually eat them put into a basin with milk and sweeted a little more with sugar and spice." In the fall came apples—"we have nowhere, to my knowledge, seen or eaten finer apples"—and peaches in such abundance that windfalls were left for the swine to feed on.

This cornucopia that travelers reported hides an unpleasant fact: the daily diet most settlers lived on was dull and tasteless, particularly in households that stuck closely to English ways of preparing food. They were not adventuresome cooks. They sampled the native sweet potato and rejected it. The white potato, also native, did not slip into the menu until the Scotch-Irish brought it into the country in the eighteenth century as the Irish potato. Cabbage was a favorite with the Dutch and Germans, who gave the land "koolslaa" and sauerkraut. They also contributed waffles, and the Dutch added two culinary words and delicacies—cookie (from the Dutch *koekje*) and cruller (from *krulle*). But settlers of English descent, at least in the seventeenth century, kept mainly to a tiresome diet handed down from their ancestors.

They brought from home an ingrained distaste for vegetables, "food more meet for hogs and savage beasts to feed upon than mankind," and a conviction that they were unhealthy when eaten raw. They planted familiar root crops in the kitchen garden—parsnips, turnips, carrots, and onions—then cooked them lovingly into something close to a tasteless pulp. Except for salt and pepper, most of the condiments also came from the garden—parsley, hyssop, thyme, marjoram, all of which they had known in England. Between a breakfast of some kind of mush diluted with milk or molasses and something similar for supper came dinner, the main meal, served anytime between noon and three o'clock. It consisted usually of a stew or pottage whose contents varied with the season. It required only a single pot and little tending, and thus imposed slight demands on the housewife. It was served as stews are today. Only in the eighteenth century and among the well-to-do did individual portions of vegetables and meat appear on plates.

Despite the resistance to change, the diet became Americanized within the first generation of settlers. First, they took from the Indians all they grew and the recipes for making it palatable. The Boston baked beans of today came from the Indians, who taught the newcomers how to cook them in earthen pots. Pumpkin, more popular then than later, was boiled and mashed and served with butter, adapted to pies, or dried in slices that kept interminably. Corn, of course, became central to the diet. Pounded into powder and called samp, it served well for breakfast, "eaten hot or cold with milk and butter," according to Roger Williams. As succotash (corn cooked with beans) it could pass for supper. There was corn on the cob for August meals, and parched corn, cooked in hot ashes and beaten into powder, which could be nibbled on like peanuts. Among the variety of dishes, the one favored in the South was hominy grits. Richard Hooker describes the recipe:

> It was made by scalding shelled corn in a kettle of water and wood ashes until the hulls separated, then winnowing and drying the grains. After washing and soaking, the corn was boiled and came from the pot soft, plump, and white. Small grained hominy, in time to be called grits, was often made into a kind of hasty pudding or dried for winter use. Served in a variety of ways—in Maryland and Virginia it was boiled with beans and milk until the whole mass became firm, after which it could be eaten hot or cold with bacon or other meat. In some places "hog and hominy"—hominy fried with pork—was favored.

A diet confined to corn can lead to pellagra. The settlers' overcooked vegetables added little to nutrition, but a second alteration in their English diet added protein that helped to keep them healthy. In England they had "white meat" (cheese) but in America they could supplement that with fish from the sea, birds from the air, and animals from the forests. The free-roaming pig quickly became the preferred source of protein. It demanded little attention and smoked, salted, or pickled was easily preserved. The pig, with its abundant fat, slowly led to new ways of cooking. The pot for stews remained omnipotent, but the frying pan through the century gained equality. Visitors from Europe found it unique to America. It was light and easy for the housewife to handle, it produced a dish quickly, and for someone on the move it was easy to carry.

The bad teeth Josselyn and everyone else found in America revealed a further characteristic of the American diet—a fondness for what the English called "sweets." Sugar was a luxury in America, but less so than in Europe because of the relative nearness to and constant trade with the West Indies. A New Englander in 1651 bartered twelve bushels of rye for a loaf of it, plus a doll and a bird whistle. It was "sold in the form of large white cones, called loaves, weighing from eight to ten pounds," Richard Hooker reports. "A sugar loaf was locked up, to be taken out as needed and cut, carefully and sparingly, with sugar shears. A family might use one loaf a year. . . . The price was steep inland, cheap on the coast." But there were substitutes—molasses for one, honey for another, maple sugar for still another. The English and Dutch imported bees—"English flies" the Indians called them—early in the century. A visitor to New York in the 1670s remarked that "you shall scarce see a house but the south side is begirt with hives of bees." The Indians taught the settlers how to tap the sugar tree, later called the maple. It yields "a kind of sap or juice which by boiling is made into sugar," said a seventeenth-century Chesapeake resident. "This juice is drawn out by wounding the trunk of the tree, and placing a receiver under the wound. It is said that the Indians make one pound of sugar out of eight pounds of the liquor. It is bright and moist with a full large grain, the sweetness of it being like of good muscovada [unrefined sugar]." Settlers resisted this native source of sweetener possibly because of the labor involved. Not until the eighteenth century did the "sugaring off" of maple trees become a common tradition.

What They Drank

The colonists disliked and distrusted water and drank it only when they had no choice. Milk, first from goats, later from cows, was a principal beverage in the North, which fenced in its cattle; in the South, where livestock roamed the woods and milk soured quickly in the hot climate, it was less favored. The settlers had no tea, coffee, or chocolate to slake their thirst; none of these beverages reached England until the mid-seventeenth century, and the colonies much later. In the beginning they had no wine or beer except what came in aboard ships. The mature wine from wild grapes was barely palatable, and years passed before hops and malts needed for beer were grown. It was said of one toper who had exhausted his supply of drink from home that he soon sank so low as to be "content with water." This is another of those exaggerations passed down through the centuries that has little root in fact. They may have found it "in no wise agreeable," but as Richard Hooker observes, "thirst, the lack or scarcity of any alternative, the extreme heat, and the presence of cold, bubbling springs—all led to making it acceptable."

Still, a livelier slaker of thirst was needed, and much energy was spent in the search of a more adequate liquid refreshment. Archaeologists have found portable stills in excavations of early Virginia compounds, and it is possible that some frantic settler early on lucked upon one more virtue of that miracle grain, corn—the mash from it could be distilled into whiskey. Wesley Frank Craven has said of Captain George Thorpe, an early Virginia leader and "a man of remarkable energies," that he "seems also to have been the first to establish the possibility of producing a satisfactory beverage from the Indian corn." (His

name inexplicably does not appear in that compendium of notable Americans, *The Dictionary of American Biography.*) An
impelling reason for the orchards that quickly graced every
farm was that the fruit they gave could be converted into a
hardy beverage. For many a settler, especially those suffering
from malaria, a dipperful of hard cider, peach brandy, or something equally invigorating on rising let the new day start on a
pleasant note.

Regardless of laws passed (and all colonies passed them) and
sermons preached, excessive drinking remained common. The
militia's "training days," a pious New Englander said, "are little
more than drinking days." Edmund Morgan gives a dreary picture of the weeks when the tobacco fleet floated about the
Chesapeake.

> Virginians crowded aboard and drank away their promises and their
> profits. Anything that smelled of alcohol would sell, and the govern-
> ment complained of the "rates which unconscionable merchants
> and mariners do impose upon our necessities . . . especially of rotten
> wines which destroy our bodies and empty our purses."

The well-to-do drank imported wines and French brandies,
but once the colonists began to produce malt and hops, beer
became the favored drink among the plain people. The Dutch,
soon after settling in, produced a hardy brew from wheat.
Breweries appeared early elsewhere—Virginia had two by
1629, Massachusetts one in 1637. Penn promised early immigrants they would find plenty of beer in Philadelphia because
an early settler—"an able man"—had built "a large brewhouse
in order to furnish the people with good drink, both there and
up and down the river." He also promised plenty of rum, made
from imported molasses, and a favorite among settlers who
liked distilled spirits. To one visitor, Manhattan Island seemed
awash in it. To a New Englander, rum was for those "that are
poor and wicked, too, [who] can for a penny or two make themselves drunk." In the Chesapeake that "diabolical liquor," ac-

cording to a contemporary, "does more mischief to people's industry than anything except gin and the Pope. . . . My dear countrymen are fonder of it than they are of their wives and children, for they often sell the bread out of their mouths to buy rum to put in their own." In New York, where the Dutch called it "kill-devil," a visitor said that "all these people are very fond of it, and most of them extravagantly so, although it is very dear and has a bad taste."

The North supplemented beer and rum with hard cider, "made by exposing the cider to freezing weather, then removing the surface ice as it formed, leaving the remainder of higher alcoholic content." The South preferred peach brandy, which was often quite good but "would have been better if it had been more carefully made." All regions liked mixed drinks, among them cider and rum, cider and mead, and, above all, flip, the recipe of which was

> beer sweetened with sugar, molasses, or dried pumpkin, and strengthened with some spirit, usually rum. Into this mixture a red-hot iron was thrust, which made the liquor foam and gave it a burned, bitter flavor.

Even by modern standards early America appeared to be what can only be called a boozy society.

Diseases

Those who seek to discuss the diseases early settlers endured move into a hazy world. Diseases change in time and vary from place to place. Influenza, notable then and now for its swift and radical mutations, presents symptoms that differ from year to year. Some historians believe that syphilis arose in Europe as a mutation of leprosy, an endemic disease there until it began to vanish in the sixteenth century. Medical scholars are reasonably certain that the settlers found no new diseases in America and that all they suffered were imported. But what afflictions did they bring with them? Malaria was one; it was not a killer but a "great debilitator" that left victims enervated for months after a seizure. Smallpox was another. It appeared early and reappeared throughout the century every ten or fifteen years as a new generation of susceptible children arrived on the scene. It led to a slow and repulsive death. William Bradford left behind a report of the suffering endured by local Plymouth Indians who caught it. "A sorer disease cannot befall them," he wrote,

> and for want of bedding and linen and other helps they fall into a lamentable condition as they lie on their hard mats, the pox breaking and mattering and running one into another, their skin cleaving by reason thereof to the mats they lie on. When they turn them[selves], a whole side will flay off at once, as it were, and they will be all of a gore blood, most fearful to behold. And . . . they die like rotten sheep.

Whites suffered equally horrible deaths. "The smallpox came out by the thousands on his face," a physician remarked of one victim, "which soon became one entire blister, and in two or three days after the body and limbs were beset with such numbers of them that the load bore down his strength before it in spite of every measure taken for his assistance."

The symptoms of malaria and smallpox make them fairly easy for the historian to identify, but other diseases are more difficult to sort out from the vague lexicon of the day. The flux, or bloody flux, indicated some bowel disorder that could be anything from diarrhea to dysentery to typhoid fever. Cancer generally meant an ulcerous spreading sore. Consumption indicated a persistent respiratory illness that could vary from tuberculosis to pneumonia. No one then died of something that was specifically diagnosed as heart disease. Convulsions, perhaps, dropsy, or apoplexy, but not heart disease.

Much of the materia medica and therapeutics of the day centered around relieving and curing a single symptom—fever. Fevers were loosely and variously identified. Intermittent fevers came and went at regular intervals. They were called agues if accompanied by chills; a tertian ague meant that the chills came every third day and generally connoted malaria. Intermittent fever left patients weak but rarely killed them. Malignant, pernicious, or putrid fevers were more dangerous and often fatal. Sometimes they were known by more specific names, such as "nervous fever" (typhoid) or "jail fever" (typhus).

A fever was cured by draining the body of the "morbific matter" that caused it. The evacuating remedy favored by physicians was bleeding. The explanation for its efficacy varied from doctor to doctor, but all, and their patients, too, generally agreed it worked wonders. Apparently they felt it had a psychological as well as physical effect, for unconscious patients were not bled. The privy was perhaps the busiest spot in the vicinity of a sick person's house, for as day followed night, so purging followed bloodletting. Purges discharged acrid feces and bile and thus "invited morbid excitement from the blood vessels to the bowels." No medicines were administered until a patient's bowels had been emptied, and if the slightest sign of costiveness appeared later, further steps were taken to keep things moving.

Many historians hold that the seventeenth century—and the eighteenth as well—favored nauseous medicines with "stinking odors" to invigorate patients' spirits. To that end "asafetida, oil of amber, burnt leather, and feathers will be used . . . [to] provide the soul with strong and disagreeable feelings." There is little evidence to back up this view. A small bag of asafetida, a foul-smelling herb commonly known as "devil's dung," might be draped about a patient's neck for a very sensible reason—to keep the person with a communicable disease at a healthy distance. Most practitioners laced unpleasant medicines with sugar, honey, or fruit juice to make them palatable. Ardent spirits and wine were also favored diluents.

The seventeenth century held that God made all things with reference to man and his needs. "We have the Scriptures to back it that God created nothing in vain," said John Josselyn, who made at least two trips to New England to study the flora and fauna there with an eye to their medicinal value. Josselyn discovered that the rough surface of green pinecones served to remove wrinkles from the face. The kidney bean was, of course, "good to strengthen the kidneys." The eggs of a turkey buzzard restored "decayed nature exceedingly." The fangs of wolves strung about the neck saved children from fright. The rattlesnake exorcized a variety of ills. Its flesh was fed to the infirm in broths; its gall, mixed with chalk and shaped into "snake balls," cured the bellyache; its oil was used in Virginia to alleviate gout and in New England for frozen limbs.

Prescriptions like these make seventeenth-century medicine look more ridiculous than it was. The practitioners of that day, be they old wives or trained physicians, were not fools. Well over a century before James Lind in 1751 prescribed lemon juice to prevent scurvy, they were dispensing similar advice. Bleeding, long ridiculed, is currently being considered as a possible preventative of heart attacks. Tobacco is still prescribed by some physicians, as it was in the seventeenth century, to aid digestion and promote regularity. Sassafras is now discredited as a cure for syphilis, but other of its virtues are celebrated in a rhyme that still circulates:

> In the spring of the year,
>   When the blood is too thick,
> There is nothing so rare
>   As the sassafras stick.
> It cleans up the liver,
>   It strengthens the heart,
> And to the whole system
>   New life doth impart.
> Sassafras, oh, sassafras!
>   Thou art the stuff for me!
> And in the spring I love to sing
>   Sweet sassafras! of thee.

Here is a folk remedy for a toothache attended with swelling:

They boil gruel of flour of maize and milk; to this they add, whilst
it is yet over the fire, some of the fat of hogs or other suet and stir
it well, that everything mix equally. A handkerchief is then spread
over the gruel and applied as hot as possible to the swelled cheek,
where it is kept till it is gone cool again.

The prescription sounds ludicrous, but a visitor admired for his
learning said of it: "I have found that this remedy has been very
efficacious against a swelling; as it lessens the pain, abates the
swelling, opens a gathering, if there be any, and procures a good
discharge of pus." Judged by its contemporaries, seventeenth-
century medicine was not to be dismissed out of hand.

The Healers

The colonies did little to oversee the practice of medicine, but
they did attempt to control fees. Virginia tried four times to
hold down "the excessive and immoderate prices exacted by
diverse, avaricious . . . practitioners in physic and surgery," but
with little success. In 1655, when a carpenter received six hundred pounds of tobacco for building a house twenty feet square,
doctors charged from a thousand to twenty-five hundred
pounds of tobacco for attending patients. Massachusetts Bay
had no more luck in reining in the doctors. The fees were
immoderate by English standards partly because of conditions
unique to America. Dispersed settlements meant that the
American physician, unlike his English colleagues, had to spend
considerable time traveling to and from patients. The miles
covered became a fixed and considerable part of his bills, an
innovation in American medical practice that lasted into the
twentieth century.

Another innovation broke more sharply with English medical
traditions. There medical practice was divided into three

branches—the physician, addressed as "doctor," who was a university graduate with a sound grounding in medical theory; the surgeon, addressed as "mister," who was considered little more than a craftsman; and the apothecary, who compounded and sold drugs. All three came to America in the early ships and tried to practice as they had at home. The cumbersome arrangement collapsed quickly, and for a simple reason—there was not enough business in the thinly populated land to keep all three fully employed. By the end of the century the American doctor served as physician to his patients, did his own surgery, and concocted his own drugs.

The colonists did not want for professional medical care. The London Company sent over physicians, surgeons, and apothecaries in the early ships to Virginia. Dr. Samuel Fuller, who had been educated at Leyden under the renowned Hermann Boerhaave, was a passenger on the *Mayflower*. New York had Dr. Adriaen Van der Donck, another former student of Boerhaave, and Connecticut had John Winthrop, Jr., son of the first governor of Massachusetts Bay. A notebook of Winthrop's dealing with his medical practice still survives, and Oliver Wendell Holmes's gloss on its contents deserves to be quoted at length for the picture it gives of seventeenth-century American medicine as exemplified by one of its ablest practitioners.

> His great remedy, which he gave oftener than any other, was nitre [saltpeter], which he ordered in doses of twenty or thirty grains to adults, and of three grains in infants. Measles, colics, sciatica, headache, giddiness, and many other ailments, all found themselves treated, and I trust bettered, by nitre; a pretty safe medicine in moderate doses, and one not likely to keep the good Governor awake at night, thinking whether it might not kill, if it did not cure. We may say as much for spermacetic, which he seems to have considered "the sovereign'st thing on earth" for inward bruises, and often prescribes after falls and similar injuries.
>
> One of the best remedies, in point of frequency, which he was in

the habit of giving, was (probably diaphoretic) antimony; a mild form of that very active metal, and which, mild as it was, left his patients very commonly with a pretty strong conviction that they had been taking *something* that did not exactly agree with them. Now and then he gave a little iron or sulphur or calomel, but very rarely; occasionally, a good, honest dose of rhubarb or jalap. . . .

The excellent Governor's accounts of diseases are so brief that we get only a very general notion of the complaints for which he prescribed. Measles and their consequences are at first more prominent than any other affliction; but the common infirmities of both sexes and of all ages seem to have come under his healing hand. Fever and ague appear to have been of frequent occurrence.

His published correspondence shows that many noted people were in communication with him as his patients. Roger Williams wants a little of his medicine for Mrs. Weekes's daughter; worshipful John Haynes is in receipt of his powders. . . . Restless Samuel Gorton, now tamed by the burden of fourscore and two years, writes so touching an account of his infirmities, and expresses such an over-flowing gratitude for the relief he has obtained from the Governor's prescriptions, wondering how "a thing so little in quantity, so little in scent, so little in taste, and so little to sense in operation, should beget and bring forth such effects," that we repent our hasty exclamation, and bless the memory of the good Governor, who gave relief to the worn-out frame of our long-departed brother, the sturdy old heretic of Rhode Island.

Winthrop represented the best in medical practice of the time. He was well-read in the literature and thoroughly acquainted with the materia medica, yet the distance between his precepts and those of folk medicine was slight. It was not beyond him to recommend a remedy, such as Dorothy Hartley describes, that dated back to medieval times:

A small and pleasant craft of the blacksmith was to remove styes from the eyes of children. They were sent to him to ask him to do it, and he'd say, "Just wait till I've done this horseshoe," and the child would push close to watch, close to the heat and the steam, and blink hard, every time the great hammer came down with a bang—till in half an hour the smith would wipe his hands, and look, and smile (for the stye had burst and wept itself away).

Two axioms guided Winthrop and the old wives: nothing got well of itself, and somewhere in nature existed a remedy to cure every illness. Neither he nor his colleagues dismissed folk medicine as quackery. Nor did the public. In 1680 the town meeting of Guilford, Connecticut, voted with only a single objection to levy a special tax to pay for the community's use of "Mrs. Corster's physic and physical drugs." It would have pleased Winthrop to learn that the discovery of digitalis by an eighteenth-century physician had emerged from an old woman's concoction of foxglove leaves.

7

THE RHYTHMS

OF LIFE

The Calendar

HE EARLY settlers marked time by a variety of calendars. The Dutch and presumably the Germans, Swedes, and anyone who had emigrated from the Continent used the Gregorian, or New Style, calendar. Those from England held to the Julian, or Old Style, calendar. This could confuse a traveler who expected to celebrate Christmas or Easter on a certain day, for the two calendars failed to jibe by ten days. (The confusion would last until 1752, when Great Britain and her colonies finally shifted to the New Style.) New England Congregationalists and Quakers in the Delaware Valley used their own versions of the Julian calendar, one stripped of its pagan heritage. They wiped away the names of the months and days of the week; Sunday, for instance, became First Day. "We under the New Testament," went the dictum, "follow God's will in acknowledging no holydays except the first day of the week only." Even Christmas, a day of revelry in England, went by the board. On Christmas Day 1621, Governor Bradford of Plymouth found the settlers "in the street at play, openly." He cut their pleasure short, and as long as he ruled the colony "nothing hath been attempted that way, at least openly." And so it was throughout New England. Holidays varied in seventeenth-century England from one part of the country to the other, but four that marked the seasons were generally accepted everywhere.

Lady's Day—March 25
Midsummer—June 24
Michaelmas—September 29
Christmas—December 25

Others such as Candlemas, Shrove Tuesday, St. Valentine's Day, Good Friday, Easter Sunday, and Whitsunweek (Whitsuntide) were also generally observed. Old customs die hard, and even in New England farmers often privately noted these days in their journals.

The Sabbath was the single day universally observed but again in various ways. A traveler, marooned in Boston on a Sunday, deplored what he saw:

> All their religion consists in observing Sunday by not working or going into the taverns on that day; but the houses are worse than the taverns. No stranger or traveler can therefore be entertained on a Sunday, which begins at sunset on Saturday and continues until the same time on Sunday. At these two hours you see all their countenances change. Saturday evening the constable goes round into all the taverns of the city for the purpose of stopping all noise and debauchery, which frequently causes him to stop his search before his search causes the debauchery to stop.

The Dutch openly practiced a Continental Sunday, one of conviviality after church. The taverns were open and everyone enjoyed the day as one made for pleasure. The Chesapeake tried in the beginning to enforce a strict Sabbath. Church attendance was required at least once a month, the grinding of corn was forbidden on the Sabbath, and the sheriff could make no arrests on that day. But the ordinances were quickly flouted, partly because of the castoffs the Bishop of London sent over as ministers. Between the times they would "babble in the pulpit" they would also "roar in the tavern, . . . and rather by their dissoluteness, destroy than feed their flocks." A pious visitor toward the end of the century found "the lives of the planters in Maryland and Virginia are very godless and profane." The trend that had set in there soon became fixed in most colonies. "Sunday is very badly kept," said a later visitor to Pennsylvania, "especially in the rural districts, where most country folk pay little attention to it."

Except on Sunday, the rhythms of daily life for men and women differed. Women were tied to the house and the farm. Their weeks, day in and day out, varied little. Always there were clothes to wash, meals to cook, children to tend. For the men, however, the seasonal calendar gave as much variety as a farmer might expect. They planted in the spring, tended fields through the summer, harvested in the fall, and when so inclined could interrupt this cycle with a trip to the gristmill or nearby tavern or take a holiday to fish or hunt. Women's routines continued through the winter, but the men's became desultory. They prepared for the next round of seasons at their own pace. They built and repaired fences. When the frozen ground made it easy to haul in timber, they did so. If in the mood, they collected ashes from a bonfire of fallen trees and boiled them down to potash, which the women converted into soap. In wet weather those who grew wheat threshed it in the barn.

Within this broad pattern, the rhythms of daily life differed little for women, north or south, but they varied radically for men. The Chesapeake farmer broke from winter with the planting of his tobacco seedbeds in February, a month earlier than the northern farmer would begin to work his fields. In October, when the northern farmer had his harvest in, the tobacco farmer was still drying his crop in the shed and would have little free time until his hogsheads were aboard ship in November or later. These varying rhythms affected the way each farmer observed the calendar. England's traditional harvest feast, a holiday not tied to the Church of England, was carried to New England and celebrated more solemnly as a feast of thanksgiving. The timing was right, for the two harvests nearly synchronized. The timing was not right for the Chesapeake and the feast there vanished from the calendar. There Christmas became the high holiday of the year, as in England a day of revelry, gift giving, partying, and often, too, a time for marrying. People not only had time to attend weddings, but (unlike in New England) travel was not difficult in a land generally free of snow and ice. Whitsunweek, which arrived the seventh Sunday after Easter, soon after the tobacco seedlings had been transplanted to the fields, presented another break from daily routine that went unacknowledged in most of the North.

Rites and Ceremonies

In the beginning and for most of the century the American calendar was the dullest in Western civilization. Few rites and ceremonies punctuated the weeks and months to distract settlers from the hardship of daily life. The settlers, from wherever they came, left behind a rich heritage of folk customs and local holidays, market days and fairs, games, songs, and dances peculiar to their village or region. Much of that heritage vanished in America. Where there were no towns or villages there could be no fairs. Traditions to which settlers from one village were accustomed often were at odds with those of new neighbors from another village. All this "reminds us how much was lost in transit," Richard L. Bushman remarks.

> Where were the morris dancers, the wassailing, the annual wakes, the crafts holidays, maypoles? Was Saint Monday observed anywhere in the colonies in the seventeenth century? . . . And what of the vocational culture of shoemakers, weavers, woodcutters, ma-

sons, herdsmen, shepherds, miners, beggars, and thieves? The great bulk of the early migrants dissolved into the farm population, and where there were craftsmen they were dispersed. One or two shoe-makers in a town could scarcely do justice to Saint Crispin's feast.

Much of the seventeenth century was spent by the settlers slowly evolving new rituals created by or shaped to a new setting.

Marriage, in England a standardized ceremony controlled by the Anglican church, took on a variety of forms in America. The steps leading to it remained fairly constant—negotiations between parents or guardians over the dowry, followed by a betrothal, or engagement as it would later be called—but the ceremony itself differed widely. The Dutch and Pennsylvania Germans performed it in their native languages. The Quakers held it in their meetinghouses, where to the astonishment of strangers a couple without benefit of clergy or any secular authority married themselves with vows often of their own devising. In the South the Anglican rite embedded in the Book of Common Prayer remained intact, but local government interjected itself into what had once been the exclusive domain of the church. Publication of the banns, which had sufficed at home to alert a village of an impending marriage, failed to work among the dispersed settlements of the Chesapeake. Some way had to be found to spread the word to all—parents, guardians, masters, and kinfolk—of the intended event, and to that end the marriage license, issued by the county clerk, was created. (By the end of the century the innovation had spread northward into the Middle Colonies.) A southern wedding was usually held in the home and was an occasion for the gathering of the neighborhood and the clan. After the minister completed the ceremony, the festivities began—card playing and dancing, followed by "an elegant supper, a cheerful glass, and the convivial song to close the entertainment."

New England departed radically from English custom. The Congregationalists held that nothing in the Bible designated marriage as a religious rite—even pagans got married—and they made it a civil affair officiated by a magistrate. It does not appear to have been an excuse for festivity but served to affirm a contract between two young people about to enter a world where they would lead lives separate from their families. It could be a casual affair, if an anecdote repeated by Arthur W. Calhoun is not apocryphal. As he tells it, a couple living out of wedlock was scandalizing a Connecticut village. One day a magistrate met them on the street.

> "John Rogers," he said, "do you persist in calling this woman, a servant younger than yourself, your wife?"
>
> "Yes, I do."
>
> "And do you, Mary, wish such an old man as this to be your husband?"
>
> "Indeed, I do."
>
> "Then by the laws of God and this commonwealth, I, as a magistrate, pronounce you man and wife."

The early New England funeral, more than the wedding, was a public, even a social, event, an occasion for the gathering of the neighborhood and clan. A minister presided over a brief, stark ceremony. After the burial, however, the mourners returned to the house where they shared a meal and spiced drinks in a more convivial atmosphere. The grave of the deceased was more often than not located on family land and marked by an unadorned stone slab. All this changed as the century progressed. Cemeteries, though often overgrown with weeds, materialized somewhere near the meetinghouse. Elaborately carved stones marked the graves. The funeral itself became an even more social event, one of the few formal rituals that New England accepted. The once modest meal after the service became a feast. The well-to-do and even those who could not afford it passed out costly gifts to those who attended—scarves, gloves, even gold rings. As John C. Miller remarks, "Funerals tended to become an opportunity for the conspicuous display of wealth even more than grief."

Something similar happened in the South. Early funerals were simple affairs. The need for haste to get the unembalmed body in the ground meant they often lacked a minister, but the Book of Common Prayer was there to guide the service. It was the custom

> to bury in gardens or orchards, where whole families lie interred together, in a spot generally handsomely enclosed, planted with evergreens, and the graves kept decently. Hence . . . arises the occasion of preaching funeral sermons in houses, where at funerals are assembled a great congregation of neighbors and friends; and if you insist upon having the sermon and ceremony at church, they'll say to you they will be without it, unless performed *after their usual custom.*

The funeral during the seventeenth century came to be an occasion for conspicuous consumption in the South, too. The postburial meal became a feast, and even "most middling people" would go into debt to have the minister give a sermon, "though it cost them a very substantial forty-shilling fee."

Conspicuous consumption but not solemnity marked other among early America's few ceremonial affairs. Fairs in northern port towns had by the end of the century, said the pious Benjamin Franklin, deteriorated into gatherings that "corrupt the morals and destroy the innocence of our youth." Similar judgments were made about muster days, when men in the militia gathered as much to drink as to rehearse the military manual. Most rituals that evolved through the century combined work with pleasure, and people of the day, if asked, would have called them frolics, their word for recreation. The husking bee—an American innovation—was a social event as much as a cooperative enterprise. While the men husked the corn, they talked about crops and weather and the predators currently killing their livestock; the women traded gossip and recipes. The bee in supposedly sedate New England, but elsewhere, too, collected young ladies in the neighborhood and their swains. "After the corn is finished, they, like the Hottentots, give three cheers or huzzas but cannot carry in the husks without a rum bottle; they feign great exertion but do nothing till rum enlivens them, when all is done in a trice, then after a hearty meal about ten at night they go to their pasttimes." A house-raising in the Delaware Valley rounded up families in the neighborhood, and again a similar festive air ruled the day.

Many of the rituals of the time were tied to politics. The annual town meeting in New England villages was as much a social event as a political affair, one of the few times of the year when all citizens gathered together. Lost to posterity are the jests, witticisms, and animosities pent up over the year that must have burst forth during these meetings; the people who have come down to the present in the formal records, by contrast, appear as dour and forbidding. Court days were the South's equivalent of the town meeting. The neighborhood gathered to watch and judge friends and acquaintances accused of crimes. They studied the list of applicants for marriage licenses posted on the county clerk's door, they paid off and collected debts, they drank, they gossiped and generally socialized.

The ritual of a court day or a town meeting gave a zest to lives with few pleasures and much hard work. Even a day at church could add a spark to what had been a dull week. In New England the double Sunday service, one in the morning, one in the afternoon, could lead to torpor, but in a village with a lively pastor who had a sense of drama they could be events looked forward to all week. But even within villages graced with pedestrian shepherds there lay interspersed between sermons enough time for the men to socialize and conduct business, the women to chat, and friends to offer a substantial dinner.

Churchgoing was also as much social as religious in the South. Those driven or urged to go arrived early and spent the time before service "giving and receiving letters of business, reading advertisements, consulting about the price of tobacco, grain, etc., and settling either the lineage, age or qualities of favorite horses." It made the day more tolerable to know that the service was fixed by the Book of Common Prayer and that tradition limited the minister to a sermon of only twenty minutes, give or take a few, to arouse the flock. After the service the congregation socialized again, "strolling around the church among the crowd"; dinner invitations were extended, and for most everyone a solemn day ended in conviviality. In a land where rites and ceremonies were few, the colonists made the most of what they had.

Recreation

"Laudable *recreations* may be used now and then," said Cotton Mather, an intense New England divine, "but I beseech you, let those recreations be used for *sauce* but not for *meat.*" One wonders if Mather would have approved of the chapter on recreation in Robert Beverley's account of Virginians at the end of the seventeenth century, wherein he gives precedence to "hunting, fishing, and fowling, with which they entertain themselves an hundred ways." These sports helped to stock family larders but more often became ends in themselves, created to break the dullness of daily routines. Hare hunts, for instance, seldom had a practical value. They began, like a fox hunt in England, with dogs. Once the hares had been chased into the hole of a dead tree

> the business is to kindle a fire, and smother them with smoke, till they let go their hold and fall to the bottom stifled, from whence they take them. If they have a mind to spare their lives, upon turn-

ing them loose they will be as fit as ever to hunt at another time, for
the mischief done them by the smoke immediately wears off.

Hunting for "vermin"—raccoons and opossums—was another
favorite Chesapeake sport. "It is perform'd afoot with small
dogs in the night by the light of the moon or stars," Beverley
reports. "Wherever the dog barks, you may depend upon
finding the game, and this alarm draws men and dogs that way."
When the prey has been treed, "they detach a nimble fellow up
after it, who must have a scuffle with the beast before he can
throw it down to the dogs, and then the sport increases to see
the vermin encounter those little curs." The young men took
special delight in hunting wild horses "foaled in the woods of
the uplands that never were in hand and are as shy as any
savage creature." They carried no brands and could thus be
claimed by their captors. "However," Beverley says, "the cap-
tor commonly purchases these horses very dear, spoiling better
in the pursuit, in which case he has little to make himself
amends besides the pleasure of the chase. And very often this
is all he has for it, for the wild horses are so swift that 'tis difficult
to catch them." And when caught they are not worth much, for
they are either old and lame or "so sullen that they can't be
tam'd."

Beverley says nothing about three spectator sports popular in
the Chesapeake and everywhere else in America—horse racing, cockfighting, and bull baiting. Bull baiting had been imported from England, where it flourished in the market towns.
One of the few surviving accounts of an American bull bait
comes from an eighteenth-century Philadelphian, but the rules
of the game had been fixed so long that what he describes,
except for the outcome, can be applied to the seventeenth
century. "The animal was in a great rage, tho' much exhausted
before I reached the scene of action," he writes. "Soon after I
got there, the bull threw a small mastiff about ten foot high,

which he hooked in the upper jaw and tore it nearly off with every tooth in it. A new pack of dogs were now prepared for the combat, and every eye was turned toward them." Here the narrative takes a dramatic turn:

> At this moment who should break through the ring suddenly but the beautiful Polly Heffernan (for that was her name). She was beholding the battle through the cracks of the high fence which closed the field on South Street, and pitying the persecuted animal she scaled it unseen by the crowd, which she pierced like a dart, and run directly up to the bull, without shoes or stockings on, her bosom bare and her ringlets of beautiful black hair flowing in wild disorder upon her neck and shoulders. Her clothing was nothing but her long shift and a white petticoat, so that if ghosts are she appeared more like a ghost than a human being.
>
> When she reached the bull, which almost immediately before was in a great rage, he dropped his ears and bowing his head as if he knew his deliverer was come, she thus accosted him:
>
> "Poor bully! And have they hurt thee? They shall not hurt thee any more," and stroking his forehead she repeated, "They shall not hurt thee any more."
>
> We multitude were confounded and dumbstruck with amazement. Not a man dared to enter the ring to save her, but all stood trembling for Polly's life. In the midst of their gaze, she darted back like an arrow from the bow, over the fence, and returned to the hospital from which she eloped and here the bait ended.

Cockfighting, also ignored by Beverley, flourished everywhere in early America—an Anglican minister recorded without remorse the fights he attended in New York—but because most surviving accounts come from the South it has mistakenly been thought to be the sport of that region alone. Bets ran high at every fight, and often tempers, too, when any hint of a fixed match surfaced; a beak coated with garlic to repulse an opponent, a shot of brandy to enhance a cock's self-confidence were tricks used by owners. The cocks were trained to kill and equipped with honed steel spurs to speed their work.

A northern visitor to the Chesapeake described a typical match.

> The little heroes appeared trained to the business and not the least disconcerted by the crowd or shouting. They stepped about with great apparent pride and dignity; advancing nearer and nearer, they flew upon each other . . . the cruel and fatal gaffs being driven into their bodies, and at times directly through their heads. Frequently one, or both, were struck dead at the first blow, but they often fought after being repeatedly pierced, as long as they were able to crawl, and in the agonies of death would often make abortive efforts to raise their heads and strike their antagonists.

Horse racing also became a ruling passion in early America. It began and remained a pastime ruled by the gentry—a Chesapeake tailor was fined one hundred pounds of tobacco for racing his horse in a contest reserved "for gentlemen only"—for they alone could afford the luxury of breeding animals for sport. The quarter horse, bred for speed over a short distance, became a Virginia specialty. Boston, New York, and Philadelphia tracks preferred steeds comfortable at longer distances. Rhode Island's famous Narragansett Pacers were "about as homely as a horse can be," Howard Russell remarks, "but their smooth, steady gait, their speed and sure-footedness, and their intelligence and stamina earned their high reputation. Their gait was a swift amble, so even that at high speed a rider could carry a pail of water without spilling."

In the winter, colonists in the South moved into the house, where dancing and card playing relieved the daily routine. Ice skating, sledding, and later, when horses became prevalent, sleighing were favorite winter sports in the North. Youngsters' sledding routines were fixed early and have changed little since. "Every boy and youth in town, from eight to eighteen," said a visitor to Connecticut at the end of the century, "had a little sledge, made with a rope, like a bridle, to the front, by which it could be dragged after one by hand." The driver would push off down the hill "as one would launch a boat, and then with the most astonishing velocity, precipitated by the weight of its owner, the little machine glided past and was at the lower end of the street in an instant."

The calendar at the end of the century remained much as it had been at the beginning—everywhere fairly stark compared to what had been known by all in Europe. Slowly, as the years passed, the settlers devised ways to escape, however briefly, the daily drudgery of carving a new life from the wilderness. Some honored the English Christmas, others the harvest feast. Here a house-raising, there ice skating or sledding, elsewhere a possum hunt enlivened dull days. But the rhythms of life differed up and down the land. At the end of the century, and for a long time afterward, the colonists in different regions celebrated nothing at the same time. Not a single rite or ceremony or holiday united them even for a moment through the year. Their calendars divided them. Those whose business took them up and down the land generally found English the common language, but not much else appeared to unify the people. Indeed, many felt as they moved along the coast that they passed through foreign lands.

8

MANNERS AND MORALS

LANGUAGE · CRIME AND PUNISHMENT · RANK AND STYLE

Language

A LANGUAGE carried into a new environment, it has been said, brings with it preconceived notions that seldom harmonize with the new setting. Indian chiefs became "kings" and their offspring "princes" and "princesses" to the early settlers. They called the bison, which then roamed along the eastern coast, the buffalo, an animal the English had heard about from Far Eastern travelers. The red-breasted thrush became the robin, though it only resembled the robin redbreast of England. The new environment can also, for a while at least, freeze language into a rigid mold. England at the time migration to America began was reminting its language—the King James Bible, published in 1611, glorified the upheaval in progress— but the isolated settlers were largely unaffected. To the new world they carried words dropping out of use at home. "Burly," "cater-cornered," "deft," "likely," "ornate," and "scant" all survived in America long after they vanished from the English scene. The word "bub" (still in use today) for "boy" died during the seventeenth century among plain people in England. In the South, blacks used "dem," "dey," and "dat," for "them," "they," and "that" not because they spoke the language slovenly but because they learned it from indentured servants fresh from England who talked that way. The dialect the blacks learned, Edward Eggleston has said, "probably preserved much that was worst in the English of the seventeenth century."

The settlers preserved more than dying words. The seventeenth-century saying "Three may keep counsel, if two be away" Benjamin Franklin later converted into "Three may keep a secret, if two of them are dead." "Fresh fish and new come guests smell by they are three days old," printed in 1670, became, in *Poor Richard's Almanac*, "Fish and visitors stink in three days." The settlers continued to rear their children on English proverbs ("Nothing succeeds like success") and English jingles ("Thirty days hath September, April, June, and November").

When the colonists came upon a new plant they gave it a short descriptive name like "popcorn" or "eggplant." Strange birds or beasts became, in new-world parlance, the bluebird, redbird, mockingbird, catbird, mudhen, the canvasback duck, the garter snake, the groundhog, the razorback hog, the flying squirrel. A tree that yielded a sap that could be boiled down to a sweet-tasting liquid became the "sugar tree" and eventually the sugar maple. Frogs of "incredible bigness" were from "the roaring they make" called bullfrogs. Two venomous vipers were dubbed the rattlesnake and the "copper bellied" or copperhead snake. "A sort of flat bug which lurks in the bedsteads and bedding and disturbs people's rest a nights" became, naturally, the bedbug. A tiny bird whose wings buzzed in flight became the "humbird."

A Frenchman complained that Americans had not "notably enriched their native language," but a people who identified an evil-smelling growth as "stinkweed" and had the sense to accept the Algonquin word "skunk" and name a foul-smelling plant "skunk cabbage," could hardly be accused of failing to enrich the language. Nor did they lack inventiveness.

"Branch," "fork," and "run" were created to designate various types of watercourses that did not exist in England. The distinctiveness of American weather called for such new terms as "cold snap" and "Indian summer." A small craft that leaped about on the water became a "catboat," and another, more graceful, became a "schooner." ("Oh, how she scoons," a Gloucesterman is supposed to have said when he saw the first one, and the name stuck.)

Curiously, the Frenchman failed to spot the number of foreign words that had by the end of the century slipped into the language, among them "chowder" (from "chaudière") and "café," then a popular word for what today would be called a barroom. The Dutch in New Amsterdam brought in a number of words—"bowery" (farm), "brief" (letter), "spook" (ghost), "scow" (riverboat), and "yacht" (boat). The front-door "stoop" was a Dutch word as well as an architectural innovation. Other contributions were "cruller" and "cookie," "boss," "dope," "lope," and "kill" (meaning "creek" and common now only in the Middle Atlantic states). Germans dropped strange words into their talk ("An old, kind Dutch landlady gave our horses for breakfast a dish of 'spelts' "), and a number of them settled into the language, such as "sauerkraut." The Scotch-Irish when they came filled the air with odd phrases that became part of the vernacular. A lady named Mrs. Ewing provided several for one traveler's journal.

"My son," says Mrs. Ewing, "lately lost his foot in the smallpox." (She meant he could not stand.)

"Will you take a check?" (She meant a late dinner.)

"Our neighbor McOlahlan since left us has flitted." (She meant has moved away.)

Then there were the Indians' contributions missed by the Frenchman. Aside from the peculiar resistance to the word "maize," the colonists took from them what their mouths could handle. The number of Indian place-names that still dominate any map of the East Coast testifies to that. They split a tongue twister like "pawschoicora" apart and brought forth "hickory." They sliced a few letters off "isquotersuash" and accepted "squash." "Arathkone" became "raccoon." Some words, like persimmon, skunk, moccasin, and canoe, and such culinary dishes as samp, pone, hominy, and succotash came into the language reasonably intact. "Wampumpeake," white shell beads that passed as currency, the settlers divided regionally into "wampum" in the North, "peake" in the South.

Regional variations, or as Franklin later put it, "some peculiar expressions familiar to its own people but strange and unintelligible to others," inevitably crept into the language. The Spanish *puma* became the mountain lion in Virginia, a tiger in South Carolina, a panther in Pennsylvania, and a catamount or cat-a-mountain in Maryland. Corn presented a problem in nomenclature that each region settled in its own way. To all, the ear of barley or wheat became the ear of corn, but the covering on the ear gave trouble. Virginians called it "shuck," New Englanders "husk," and others "trash." The core of the ear only gradually came to be called the corn cob.

Slowly through the century something that could be called an American language took shape. A visitor who asked a man how he felt got for an answer, "Oh, mighty weak." The word "mighty" set the visitor off. "It is very much in fashion in this country, and its use is sometimes ridiculous, as in this instance." (He might have mentioned the equally overused word "figure," as in, "I figure I'll make out.") Now and then social conditions affected the language. A seventeenth-century immigrant preferred to be called a "hired servant" to distinguish himself from an indentured servant, and this in time was altered to "hired hand" or simply "hand." And hands came to expect from those who hired them "room and board." Such words and phrases were not the language of the King James Bible, but, the Frenchman's judgment aside, they contributed to what would become

a rich and original way of expressing the experience of a new
land.

Crime and Punishment

"A general corruption hath overgrown the virtues of this latter
times," an Englishman remarked on the eve of colonization,
"and the world is become a brothel house of sin." Drunkenness
was endemic and robbery common. "I have seldom seen the
world at so low an ebb." The ecclesiastical courts overflowed
with cases of "adultery, whoredom, incest" and other "uncleanness and wickedness of life," and the people came to call them
"bawdy courts."

Compared to those in the England left behind, the settlers
led relatively sedate lives, but "wickedness did grow and break
forth" in early America, and William Bradford did not blink the
fact in his history of Plymouth Plantation. Sexual offenses occurred—"not only incontinency between persons unmarried,
for which many both men and women have been punished
sharply enough, but some married persons also. But that which
is worse, even sodomy and buggery (things fearful to name)
have broke forth in this land oftener than once." The most
horrifying case involved a teenage lad who "was detected of
buggery and indicted for the same, with a cow, two goats, five
sheep, two calves, and a turkey." After he had confessed, Bradford went on,

> accordingly he was cast by the jury and condemned, and after ex-
> ecuted about the 8th of September, 1642. A very sad spectacle it
> was. For first the mare and then the cow and the rest of the lesser
> cattle were killed before his face, according to the law, Leviticus xx.
> 15; and then he himself was executed. The cattle were all cast into
> a great and large pit that was digged of purpose for them, and no
> use made of any part of them.

The New Englanders depended on biblical injunctions to guide their definitions of capital crimes. Rape, however, when it came to light in 1642 in Massachusetts Bay, presented a problem. The case concerned the nine-year-old daughter of a pious settler. She had, the record reads, "grown capable of man's fellowship and took pleasure in it" with three of her father's servants. English common law defined rape as a sexual act performed with a girl under the age of ten with or without her consent or with a girl over ten without her consent. The punishment was death. The Massachusetts authorities were in a quandary, for the more tolerant Mosaic law demanded only a heavy fine levied against the man and marriage with his victim. They fined the leading offender, slit and seared his nostrils, and for the next decade forced him to wear "an hempen rope about his neck." They let the other two offenders off with fines and whippings. But shortly thereafter rape became a capital crime in Massachusetts Bay, as it was elsewhere in America.

Biblical law gave further trouble. On the authority found in Leviticus and Deuteronomy, the Massachusetts code held that "if any person committeth adultery with a married or espoused wife, the adulterer and adulteress shall surely be put to death." All regarded adultery "a most foul and filthy sin." It offered grounds for divorce by the injured party and demanded public humiliation of the offenders, but no one seems to have felt the act called for a sentence of death.

Seventeenth-century America limited the death sentence mainly to the crimes of murder, sodomy, witchcraft, and insurrection. There was no attempt to make execution for these crimes painless. When at the end of the century New York found Jacob Leisler and a cohort guilty of insurrection, they were sentenced to be drawn and quartered, which meant "to be hanged by the neck and, being alive, their bodies be cut down to the earth, that their bowels be taken out and they being alive, burnt before their faces, that their heads shall be struck off and their bodies cut in four parts."

Such a sentence makes the settlers appear barbaric. Slander, or defamation of character, an offense later centuries would treat as a misdemeanor, could be punished with a harshness that can only stun a modern reader. A Virginian found guilty in 1624 of uttering "base and detracting" remarks against the governor was ordered to

> be disarmed and have his arms broken and his tongue bored through with an awl. [He] shall pass through a guard of forty men and shall be butted by every one of them, and at the head of the troop kicked down and footed out of the fort; that he shall be banished out of James City and the island, that he shall not be capable of any privilege of freedom of the country, and that before he go out of the island he shall put in sureties of £200 for the good behavior.

Such sentences must be put in the context of the times. Slander was a serious offense with a people ripped from ancient traditions and forced to build a new society on shaky foundations. Edmund Morgan speaks for Virginia but puts it well for all early America when he remarks that the authorities of the day treated slander hard because they "recognized the fragility of the web and did everything they could to bolster the mutual respect that made it possible for people to live peaceably together." The records, north and south, are filled with women hauled before the court for calling others "a lousy slut," "a filthy old bawd," "a bitch." Invariably they were reprimanded and, the case proven, often fined, and sometimes whipped. Colonial women, it has been noted, asserted their aggressiveness "verbally through slander and defamation rather than physically, through assault and battery," but the records also show that the men were not above, or below, verbal assault. They also show that they were punished with an equally even and harsh hand.

Aside from slander, the most prevalent offense against society was drunkenness, endemic throughout early America. Even in supposedly sedate Salem, Massachusetts, it ranked first among

cases dealing with males in the local court. More often than not
such cases were tied to accusations of assault and battery or
breaches of the peace. The authorities, often topers themselves,
dealt with them tolerantly, up to a point, as if they sensed the
offenders were within the grip of an addiction, even a disease.
An early Virginia law held that the accused, the first time he
appeared in court, was "to be reproved privately by the minister, the second time publicly, the third time to lie in the bolts
[the stocks] twelve hours, . . . and if he continue in that vice, to
undergo such severe punishments as the governor and council
of the estate shall think fit to be inflicted on him." Courts in the
North seem to have been no less understanding.

Tolerance, even compassion, more than meanness, seems to
have pervaded colonial treatment of those who insulted the
community's sensibilities. A modern psychologist might be
offended by the way early Virginia dealt with a prickly case, but
given the time and place and lack of experience of those who
had to judge, the decision seems thoughtful and fair. The case
dealt with a young person who had been reared in England by
his parents as a girl. In his late teens he moved to London, had
his hair cut short, donned male clothes, and enlisted in the
army. When twenty-four and a civilian again, he came to Virginia dressed as a woman. Then one day it was found that "he
did lie with a maid of Mr. Richard Bennett's called *Great Bess.*"
A physician examined him, ruled he was a hermaphrodite and
that he should "go clothed in man's apparel, only his head be
attired in a coif and crosscloth with an apron before him. And
he shall find sureties for his good behavior."

Colonial justice shared the best and worst of what the settlers
had known in England. It was open, and verdicts tended to
reflect the feeling of the community. It was swift and simple.
Few of the magistrates and justices of the peace had legal training. The best were guided by intelligence, common sense, and
experience, but even the worst knew that decisions shaped by
flagrant prejudice would be reproved by the community. The

severity of the punishment meted out varied with the defend-
ant's record: first-time offenders generally received light sentences; repeaters were treated more harshly. Except for capital
crimes, early America avoided jail sentences. Incarceration
meant the public must maintain the prisoner during the length
of his sentence. It also meant he could not support his family
while in jail. Finally, to isolate a miscreant from society obviated
the central point of the punishments the seventeenth century
meted out—to humiliate the offender publicly. Let him instead,
before the eyes of the community, endure the pillory or the
stocks, let him suffer lashes at the whipping post. "After the
realization of his infamy had sunk in," John C. Miller remarks,
"he was expected to change his erring ways and become a
respectable member of the community. The punishment, in
short, was expected to work in his own reformation."

A central flaw in the punishments invoked, as in England, was
the prevalence of a double standard. A married man who committed adultery with a single woman usually got off lightly with
a fine, while the woman's reputation could be ruined forever.
A woman who bore an illegitimate child might be whipped
publicly, while the man only paid a fine and promised to support the child. An ordinary citizen condemned to time in the
stocks must sit while serving his sentence, but a gentleman, to
preserve his dignity, had the privilege of standing. Plain people
had to endure public whippings, gentlemen almost invariably
were excused from such humiliations. Social position determined the quality of justice. The problem in early America was
to figure out what a person's social position was.

Rank and Style

John Winthrop, a gentleman at home, stated the facts of life as
he saw them not long after coming to America: "God Almighty
in His most holy and wise providence hath so disposed of the
condition of mankind as in all times some may be rich, some

poor, some high and eminent in power and dignity, others mean and in subjection." Hundreds of years of experience had taught every Englishman to know his place in society. The ablest and most ingenious could escape from the niche God had handed them, as had Winthrop's father; most ended in the rank where they had been born.

The English determined rank in various ways—by lineage, education, professional training, and by wealth. A poor but bright lad could rise into the upper class through the church. John Smith escaped from a yeoman background by becoming an officer in a foreign army; he returned home able to sign his name "Capt. John Smith, Gent." University-trained lawyers and physicians could do the same. But few such gentlemen came to early America and fewer still of the landed gentry. Most of the immigrants were of the "middling sort." Even wealth could no longer determine a man's rank, for the distance between rich and poor through much of the seventeenth century was slight compared to what existed in England. Somehow in this unique situation ways had to be found to preserve old traditions of rank and place, otherwise an orderly society would collapse into chaos.

The settlers kept old forms and titles but distributed them differently. As in England, a farmer's spouse was known as "goodwife," or informally as "goody," and her husband as "goodman." But if Goodman Jones were chosen to be a justice of the peace, which could not have happened in England, he became "Mister Jones." If he progressed to a higher office, he might sign the record as "Mr. Jones, Esq." and his wife thereby dared to call herself "madam." America lacked a professional army, but every colony had local militias. A colonel or captain, often elected by his troops, accepted his rank as entry into the gentry, and everyone addressed him by his title. Many of the legislators who passed as gentlemen were, according to a contemporary, no more than "plain, illiterate husbandmen whose views seldom extended farther than . . . the little interests of the particular counties which they were chosen to represent."

Regardless of how they got within the chosen circle, all had the privilege "to take upon them the garb of gentlemen, by wearing gold or silver lace, or buttons, or points at their knees, or to walk in great boots." What people wore defined their social position, and every colonial government tried with sumptuary legislation to keep class lines clear. The first session of the Virginia House of Burgesses in 1619 legislated "against excess apparel" among plain people and ordered that offenders be fined by their local parishes. Massachusetts Bay early on urged the churches to stem the rise of a "great disorder general through the country in costliness of apparel, and following new fashions."

Admonitions against excess apparel did not mean that settlers were expected to dress somberly. The "best clothes" donned for Sunday and formal occasions might be of dark material, but daily garb ran the spectrum of colors. Russet was favored, at least in New England, but reds, yellows, blues, and greens were also common. For daily wear men wore a doublet, or close-fitting jacket, over a linen shirt, breeches that came down below the knees, long heavy stockings and, depending on the season and weather, either moccasins or laced leather boots. A woman's daily gown consisted, as John Demos describes it, "of three separate parts: a skirt, a bodice, and a pair of sleeves which were tied into the bodice armholes and covered by shoulder pieces called 'wings.' " Undergarments could number up to five, again depending on the weather and season. Children were dressed as "miniature adults" from about the time they could walk.

The lively colored outfits of the first settlers became more subdued as men moved into the backcountry. As James Axtell has remarked, "Colonial woodsmen quickly found that for stalking wild game or enemies—or being stalked—red coats, blue trousers, and yellow waistcoats were signal failures. Far better were the forest's natural dull shades of brown and green." Moccasins were the preferred form of footwear. They were easy to make, easy to repair, "quickly winterized by stuffing them with deer's hair, dry leaves, or grass, and as silent as the deer from whose skin they were made." They could not be waterproofed but once wrung out dried quickly over a fire. Linen shirts and woolen breeches were favored over a buckskin outfit because when wet, buckskin "sticks to the skin, and is very uncomfortable, requires time to dry, with caution to keep it to its shape."

The bulk of the plain people paid little attention to fashion. They could not afford to. They were too busy working to survive. Also, clothing was expensive and most had to buy it or the cloth from which to make it. Through three quarters of the seventeenth century few homes had a spinning wheel to make thread or a loom to convert it into cloth. Whatever clothing a family acquired had to be durable enough to pass along to the generation coming up. The fashion for underwear passed by plain people when it came in at the end of the century. Long after gentlemen had affected the handkerchief, the farmer continued to wipe his nose on his sleeve. But if, as the years passed, he prospered and he had an ambitious wife, his attitude toward dress changed. As Fernand Braudel has remarked, "Nothing has ever been effective against the passion to move up in the world," and if a change in dress could mark a change in station, then let it be pursued. Sumptuary legislation had no effect on such deep-seated drives, especially when men were pushed by their wives. Massachusetts Bay failed to impose restraints on apparel mainly because, as the leaders soon saw, the wives of local church leaders were "in some measure partners in the general disorder."

Wives of the well-to-do, abetted by their husbands, imposed their standards of proper dress upon their children. A youngster of ten from New York heading for a New England boarding school at the end of the seventeenth century carried along the following items; Alice Morse Earle, who resurrected the list, thinks it was only "a summer outfit," since it holds little "scarcely warm enough for New England winters."

11 new shirts	3 pair silver buttons
4 pair laced sleeves	2 pair fine blue stockings
8 plain cravats	1 pair fine red stockings
4 cravats with lace	4 white handkerchiefs
4 striped waistcoats with black buttons	2 speckled handkerchiefs
	5 pair gloves
1 flowered waistcoat	1 stuff coat with black buttons
4 new osenbrig [heavy linen] britches	1 cloth coat
	1 pair blue plush britches
1 gray hat with a black ribbon	1 pair serge britches
1 gray hat with a blue ribbon	2 combs
1 dozen black buttons	1 pair new shoes
3 pair gold buttons	

silk and thread to mend his clothes

Braudel has suggested that a change in the way people dress stems from more than the desire of an uppity lower class to move upward, that more is sought than prestige and status, that perhaps a new fashion is welcomed as "a new language to discredit the old, a way in which one generation can repudiate the old." Given this insight, it comes as no surprise that the young seem to have initiated new fashions in seventeenth-century America. Early male settlers favored a close-cropped hairstyle. Students at Harvard, as remarked earlier, repudiated that style and began to grow their hair long; their elders soon accepted the fashion. At the end of the century the young tired of that fashion, shaved their heads and donned periwigs. When in 1701 Samuel Sewall, an eminent Bostonian, heard that the son of a friend had "last night . . . cut off his hair (a very full head of hair) and put on a wig," he visited the lad and his parents. He told the boy that John Calvin and the ministers of Massachusetts condemned such foppery. The boy hemmed and hawed, but "seem'd to say would leave off his wig when his hair was grown

. . . to cover his ears." A few years earlier long hair had been deplored; a few years later gentlemen throughout America accepted as fact that the periwig set gentlemen apart from the meaner sort. It was expensive to buy and expensive to keep in shape. It had become the fashion even in distant Chesapeake by the end of the century. "We were accustomed to look upon what were called *gentle folks* as being of a superior order," a man reared among the plain people of the Chesapeake remarked later.

> For my part, I was quite shy of them, and kept off at a humble distance. A *periwig,* in those days, was a distinguishing badge of *gentle folk*—and when I saw a man riding the road near our house, with a wig on, it would so alarm my fears and give me such a disagreeable feeling, that, I dare say, I would run off as for my life. Such ideas of the differences between *gentle* and *simple* were, I believe, universal among all of my rank and age.

Still, even with periwigs, lines of rank could never be clearly or finely drawn in seventeenth-century America. These people, said a royal governor who knew the Chesapeake, "know too well from whence they come, and the ordinary sort of planters [who] have land of their own, though not much, look upon themselves to be as good as the best of them." The society remained too open, compared to what had been known in England, to be fixed by rigid guidelines. Colonels and privates who met on muster days would later play billiards together. The justice of the peace and the local drunkard often ended up attending a cockfight as companions or sharing a bet on a horse race. In the end neither dress, lineage, education, nor even political position determined a man's social rank. Wealth, more than anything else, set men apart.

9

RED, WHITE, AND BLACK

THE INDIAN · THE INDENTURED SERVANT · THE SLAVE

The Indian

NO SUBJECT has created more dissension among historians than the seventeenth century's treatment of the Indian. Francis Jennings ended his research of Indian-white relations in New England with "a strong aversion toward the Puritan gentry." They reneged on solemn pledges, broke treaties, and in an early version of total war did not hesitate to annihilate entire tribes. Alden Vaughan, on the other hand, covering the same ground and using much the same evidence, found New England leaders "humane, considerate, and just" toward the Indian and that they "had a surprisingly high regard for the interests of a people who were less powerful, less civilized, less sophisticated, and—in the eyes of New England colonists—less godly." Where, between these extreme views, does the truth or something close to it lie?

First, let it be noted that the white man came with good if wrongheaded intentions. The London Company's early directives insisted that settlers treat the Indians humanely, that first they must be brought into the Christian fold, next their "naked misery" relieved with civilized food and clothing, and finally that they should be trained "by gentle means to those manual arts and skills which they so much affect and do admire to see in us." They were, in short, to be brought as equal members into the English community, where they would be "most friendly welcome to conjoin their labors with ours and shall enjoy equal privileges with us." New England leaders issued similar injunctions, and William Penn did the same in the Delaware Valley. Efforts were made up and down the coast to protect the Indians from the on-pressing white man. To shield them from a weakness for alcohol, laws forbade the selling of spirits to them. In most settlements the white man at least went through the motions of purchasing the land, though the Indian seldom understood what was happening. Much has been made of the sharp bargain the Dutch drove to get Manhattan Island; it is usually forgotten that despite the cheap price they did purchase the island.

The settlers' well-meaning but wrongheaded intentions stemmed from the misconception that the Indian was a barbarian—a cultural bias not unique to the English. The word *barbarian,* Fernand Braudel has observed, is a figure of speech. "A barbarian to a Greek was anyone who was not Greek, to a Chinaman anyone not Chinese," and, it follows, to an Englishman anyone not English. They eat "like brute beasts," the early explorer Martin Frobisher reported. "They neither use table, stool, or tablecloth for comliness, but when they are embrued with blood knuckle-deep, and their knives in like sort, they use their tongues as apt instruments to lick them clean, in doing whereof they are assured to lose none of the victuals." Early settlers expanded Frobisher's disparagement of table manners to condemn the entire Indian culture. They are "bad people," went a typical comment, "having little of humanity but shape, ignorant of civility or arts, or religion; more brutish than the beasts they hunt, more wild and unmanly than that unmanned wild country, which they range rather than inhabit." Roger Williams, a true friend of the Indian who dealt honorably with

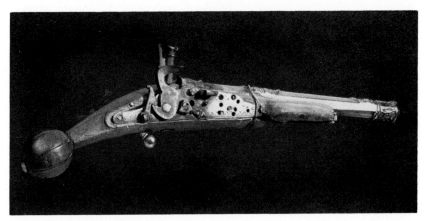

The pistol here, made of iron, brass, and steel, and most likely in seventeenth-century England, called for a long match or fuse to ignite the powder. Used by a mounted soldier, it had first to be loaded with coarse powder, a ball rammed down the barrel, then another charge of fine powder placed in the flashpan that, when ignited, sent the ball on its way. *(Pilgrim Society, Plymouth, Mass.)*

This helmet was made in England sometime between 1600 and 1630 of steel and wrought iron. *(Massachusetts Historical Society, Boston)*

This black ash rope bed, made sometime after 1670, has been identified as "the only known bedstead of any form to survive from seventeenth-century New England." The pressure of the ropes kept the tenons pressed into their mortises. Traces of red paint suggest its original color. *(Museum of Fine Arts, Boston)*

This chair, built in 1652 in Dedham, Massachusetts, survives as the earliest of dated New England furniture. The enclosed area beneath the seat was often used to secret a chamber pot, though it has been suggested that the owner of this particular chair, a schoolmaster, perhaps stored books there. The side panels beneath the arms served to keep out drafts. *(Dedham Historical Society)*

A leather-covered chair made between 1660 and 1680 of red oak and soft maple, probably in sufficient quantity—at least fifty such chairs survive—to export throughout New England and to other colonies. However, this is one of three that survive with the original upholstery. *(Museum of Fine Arts, Boston)*

A cock's-head hinge. This wrought-iron door hinge was made in England before 1660 and imported for Thomas Pynchon's ostentatious house in Springfield. *(Connecticut Valley Historical Museum, Springfield, Mass.)*

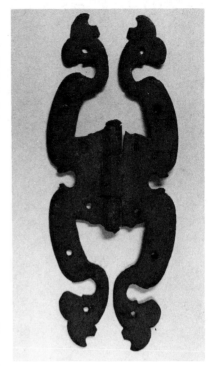

This chest was made in London, 1670, of sealskin, calfskin, gilt brass, iron, and tinned iron. *(Essex Institute, Salem, Mass.)*

A joined door made of oak, probably in Salem, Massachusetts, sometime after 1650. The original oak panels have been replaced by cheaper pine. *(Essex Institute, Salem, Mass.)*

This lantern clock, so named because it resembled a lantern, was probably made in England around 1660 and brought to New England about that time. Few, even among the wealthiest of the early settlers, owned such an elaborate mechanism. *(Wadsworth Atheneum, Hartford, Conn.)*

This elaborate brass box was made in Sheffield, England, in 1655. It was used to hold steel-nibbed pens with their quills. *(Colonial Williamsburg Foundation)*

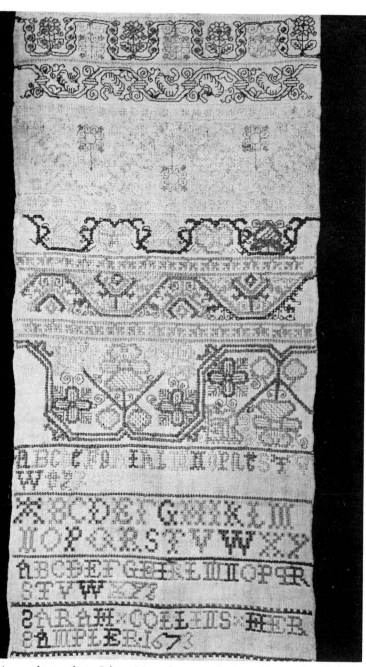

A sampler made in Salem, Massachusetts, of silk and linen, 1673.
(Henry Francis du Pont Winterthur Museum, Winterthur, Del.)

Examples of rail fencing, drawn by an Italian visitor to New England in the 1780s. *(New York Public Library)*

This cupboard, designed to store liquor and textiles, was probably built in the 1670s. According to Philip Zea, "the carving style of the cupboard is a hybridized product of second-generation craftsmen who drew on an amalgam of traditions, not necessarily English, to furnish the households of their prosperous neighbors." *(New York Public Library)*

Death's-head tombstones from a burial ground in Wethersfield, Connecticut, dating from the mid- to late-seventeenth century. *(Photographs by Carole Herbin)*

them, said "their treacheries exceed Machiavelli's." Cotton Mather, a severe man, called them "pernicious creatures," but even the gentle eighteenth-century botanist John Bartram said, "Unless we bang the Indians stoutly, and make them fear us, they will never love us, nor keep the peace long with us."

The Indian, of course, was not a barbarian. He had a culture (or rather cultures, for just as Indians differed as much physically as white men, so too did they differ culturally) as complex and deep-rooted as any European's. "The Indian population," T. H. Breen writes,

> was divided into scores of self-contained tribal groups and bands—best described as ethnic groups—that spoke languages virtually unintelligible to members of other tribes, sometimes even to those living in close proximity. These groups shared no common kinship system. The Hurons of Southern Ontario and the Creeks of the southeast, for example, were agricultural and matrilineal. Most hunting tribes of the Great Lakes area were patrilineal, but significant exceptions can be found to any relation between economy and kinship.

No single response marks the Indian attitude toward the white man, Breen goes on. "The Pequots, Powhatans, and Yamasees —just to cite familiar examples—resisted white advance and were destroyed. The Iroquois balanced competing European interests so successfully that their famed league endured long after other tribes had disappeared. The Piscataway of Maryland accommodated themselves . . . and managed not only to remain alive but also to preserve their cultural integrity."

The white man took from the Indian what he could use. The Indian paths through the woods eventually became the settlers' ways and roads. Like the natives, they girdled trees to open up the forest to sunlight. They planted, harvested, and cooked native crops as the Indians did. The Indian taught them how to use snowshoes, how to convert animal pelts into warm winter clothing, how to make a dugout canoe and a pair of moccasins.

(He did not, William Cronon and others have pointed out, show the colonists how to fertilize their cornfields with fish, despite "the legendary role of the Pilgrims' friend Squanto in teaching colonists this practice," which originated in England.) These borrowings helped to speed the white man's adjustment to the strange new world but did not fundamentally alter his culture.

On the other hand, what the Indian took from the Europeans, along with the diseases he caught from them, all but shattered his way of life. The knife or ax he yearned for, the cotton shirt, woolen blanket, the iron pot, and above all the gun and alcohol made him a cultural prisoner. Where once he hunted and trapped only when the need arose, now he traveled long distances collecting furs to exchange for the white man's goods. The French, Dutch, and Spanish all used gifts to bribe tribes within their spheres of influence to attack their European rivals. Drink was a favorite bait. "Although it is forbidden to sell the drink to the Indians, everyone does it," a visitor to New York reported, and what he saw there occurred everywhere in early America. "They immediately set about getting hold of him, giving him rum to drink, whereby he is soon caught and becomes half a fool. If he should then buy anything, he is doubly cheated in the wares, and in the price. He is then urged to buy more drink, which they now make half water, and if he cannot drink it, they drink it themselves. They do not rest until they have cajoled him out of all his money, or most of it."

The Indian's congenital weakness for drink nurtured a general contempt among settlers, but a deep prejudice can rarely be traced to a single cause. The Indian's loyalty to his culture had by the end of the century come to enrage most whites. Few of the native Americans showed any desire, Breen remarks, "to live in stuffy cabins, attend white schools, give up traditional religious practices, copy English government, adopt European medicines, or, much to the white colonists' amazement, make love to white women." Most shocking of all, many whites captured by the Indians found the new way of life so congenial they often had to be forced to return to colonial society. Without looking at themselves and their own resistance to change, the English had expected the Indian to be "essentially malleable material open to the shaping influence of a high culture and especially of the Christian religion." He proved no more malleable than they. His prodigal, un-English use of the land vexed many. Few in the seventeenth century called him a red man— the color of his skin varied from off-white to tawny to dark brown—yet regardless of the hue, skin color shaped judgments. A few Indians did try to leap the chasm between cultures. They learned English, converted to Christianity, adopted the white man's kitchen garden, fruit orchards, penned-in livestock, and other ways of farming. Rarely, if ever, were they accepted into the community except as second-class citizens. Racial prejudice in the form of anti-Indianism seems to have prevailed, even among the Quakers, who seldom tried to remake the Indian into the white man's image.

But even among those free of racial prejudice the Indian way of waging war raised fury. In 1622, without warning, the tribes of Virginia rose and killed 347 settlers over a hundred-mile area. Those who survived, once they had buried the dead, exulted. They now had reason to exterminate Satan's emissaries, who stood in the path of civilization.

> Because our hands, which before were tied with gentleness and fair usage, are now set at liberty by the treacherous violence of the savages, not untying the knot but cutting [it], so that we who hitherto have had possession of no more ground than their waste and our purchase at a valuable consideration to their own contentment, gained; may now by a right of war and law of nations, invade the country and destroy them who sought to destroy us.

Similar reactions followed after a second Indian onslaught in 1644, and from that time on the Indians were never a serious menace in the Chesapeake. Pious New England took its Indian uprising in 1675, King Philip's War, as reason to "extirpate the enemy in holy war."

Much has been written which holds that after the first third of the century white settlers carried out a conscious criminal conspiracy to exterminate the Indian and that America ever since has been forced to bear a burden of guilt for what the past did to an innocent people. There is another view. "The American aborigine was the victim of a process," Bernard W. Sheehan has written in a perceptive essay on Indian-white relations in early America. "The crime, if there was one, was the inexorable breakdown of the native's cultural integrity, in part the result of conscious policy and in part the inevitable consequence of competition between two disparate ways of life."

Sheehan's judgment echoes that of Robert Beverley, who in 1705 published the first sympathetic study of Indian culture. Beverley ended his lengthy account about the way of life among Chesapeake Indians—"their dress . . . management of children . . . cookery and food . . . war and peace . . . concerning religion . . . diseases and cures . . . handicrafts"—with words that are hard to improve on nearly three centuries later:

> They have on several accounts reason to lament the arrival of the Europeans, by whose means they seem to have lost their felicity as well as their innocence. The English have taken away great part of their country and consequently made everything less plenty amongst them. They have introduced drunkenness and luxury amongst them, which have multiplied their wants and put them up to desiring a thousand things they never dreamt of before.

The Indentured Servant

About a third of those who emigrated to northern colonies in the seventeenth century came as servants. In the Chesapeake the ratio was even higher—above 40 percent. There were exceptions, but most of these young men and women came from the working class and had few skills. Why did they come? Richard S. Dunn gives a succinct answer: "Push was more important than pull."

> The combination of hard times at home and labor demand in the colonies, facilitated by a well-organized servant trade in the chief English port towns, drew thousands of people who knew little or nothing of the Chesapeake or the Caribbean into emigration abroad. Only such an explanation can explain why English laborers flocked in great numbers to Virginia and Barbados at a time when disease, mortality rates, and agricultural working conditions were so disadvantageous to newcomers.

In 1656 John Hammond, who had lived for twenty-one years in the Chesapeake, published a pamphlet on the region, and in it he gave advice to the young man or woman who would go to America as an indentured servant. Expect, he said, to give four or five years servitude to whomever pays for your passage over the ocean. Above all, make sure you have a "contract in writing" that details the terms of your servitude, "for if ye go over upon promise made to do this or that, . . . it signifies nothing." Thomas Hellier did not heed Hammond's advice, if he knew of it. In 1677, aged twenty-seven, of a respectable family and good education, he had trifled his life away and decided to make a new start in America. In a London tavern he met a man who said he could arrange passage to the Chesapeake country. Hellier said that he "had heard so bad a character of that country that I dreaded going thither," that he was no farmer and, indeed, "I abhorred the ax and the hoe." The man *promised* "I should be only employ'd in merchants' accompts and such employments to which I had been bred." In Virginia a land speculator paid for his passage and received a headright of fifty acres of land for doing so. He then resold Hellier's indenture contract to a farmer who *promised* "me I should be employed in teaching his children and not be set to any laborious work unless necessity did compel now and then merely for a short spurt."

Instead, he found himself every day in the fields with a hoe in hand. Worse, an "ill-tongued mistress" exacerbated the misery. She "would not only rail, swear and curse me within doors, whenever I came into the house, casting on me continually biting taunts and bitter flouts, but like a live ghost would impertinently haunt me when I was quiet in the ground at work." Hellier absconded, only to be caught and returned to his master and baiting mistress. Soon thereafter he took an ax and murdered master, mistress, and a servant girl who happened in on the bloody scene. Nine months after arriving in Virginia he was hanged.

Even if Hellier had read Hammond's pamphlet he would have been misled about what to expect as a servant in the Chesapeake. Hammond said nothing about the appalling death rate among newcomers. Instead, he remarked that they would be worked less hard than in England. "Little or nothing is done in winter time; none ever work before sun rising nor after sun set; in the summer they rest, sleep, or exercise themselves five hours in the heat of the day. Saturday's afternoon is always their own, the old holidays are observed, and the Sabbath spent in good exercise." He did warn that the so-called custom of the country, a gift of fifty acres of land to the freed servant, "is an old delusion." Expect no more when your bondage ends than "a year's provision of corn, double apparel, tools necessary." True, not much to start a man down the road, but no matter, for even in bondage a man could gain "a competent estate" if he be industrious.

> There is no master almost but will allow his servant a parcel of clear ground to plant some tobacco in for himself, which he may husband at those many idle times he hath allowed him and not prejudice, but rejoice, his master to see it; which in time of shipping he may lay out for commodities, and in summer sell them again with advantage, and get a sow-pig or two, which anybody almost will give him; and his master suffer him to keep them with his own, which will be no charge to his master, and with one year's increase of them may

purchase a cow-calf or two, and by that time he is for himself. He may have cattle, hogs, and tobacco of his own, and come to live gallantly; but this must be gained (as I said) by industry and affability, not by sloth nor churlish behavior.

In the Chesapeake a servant could garner a small estate, as Hammond said, but only with his master's consent. Less depended on his industry than on his luck in the draw of a master. Laws forbade masters to "abuse their servants there with intolerable oppression and hard usage," but they usually went unenforced. Only a bold young man dared confront an abusive master in court, knowing that if the case went against him he must return to an isolated farm where his master (in Hellier's case his mistress) could treat him as he wished with little fear of outside interference. The master's power was all but absolute. He could rent out the servant, buy and sell him like "any other *commodities.*" He could bequeath him as private property. During his years of bondage the servant was in effect a slave with no real rights. He had come into a strange world as a solitary individual with no family ties to sustain or protect him. If he survived bondage he often had to hire himself out to another master. Even then he was still not treated as a first-class citizen but had to carry a certificate of freedom to assure the inquisitive that he was not a runaway. When he acquired land, as many did, he carried indelible scars that would shape his own conduct as a master. Former servants who became small planters, it has been said, "were persons who learned about proper forms of behavior, about acceptable patterns of human relations, about exploitation and competition, about 'careless resolute blows' and embittering frustrations, while they were servants." Perhaps even Hellier, if he had survived, would have been transformed into an "aggressive, competitive, highly individualistic" Chesapeake farmer.

Hellier to an extent typified the Chesapeake indentured servant. Three quarters of them were male, single, and young—

the age span varied from about sixteen to twenty-seven years. They ran the spectrum of English society up to the gentry (even a few benighted gentlemen arrived under indenture contracts), but the bulk were unskilled agricultural laborers, and here Hellier differed. His background left him unequipped for the brutality of Chesapeake life. What would have been the outcome if he had landed instead at a port town in the North? There injunctions from the church, a respect for education, and the watchful eyes of neighbors often imposed restraints on a master's conduct toward servants. Treat them as you would your children, urged John Cotton in 1655—"give them [both] the liberty and authority you would have them use, and beyond that stretch not the tether; it will not tend to their good nor yours." The laws invariably linked the treatment of servants with that of children. Both, ran an article in the Duke's Laws of New York in 1665, shall "be instructed in religion," and if either shall be "rude or worse" let the constable "inflict corporal punishment not exceeding ten stripes, provided they be of sixteen years of age."

Granted that laws and leaders in the North sought to, and often did, protect the bonded servant, his well-being still depended much on the luck of the draw. Good masters begot good freedmen. But how well were former servants equipped to enter a free life? They had learned to girdle trees, to build fences, to hoe fields of corn, wheat, or tobacco. What else? Massachusetts law held that a servant who had served his master "diligently and faithfully . . . shall not be sent away empty." What did that mean? He could survive only if he had land of his own to farm, and neither the North nor South ensured him that at the end of his bondage. He had been trained to no craft or trade, as an apprentice was trained in England, and thus had no alternatives. For most the single choice was to become a hired hand; if thrifty, diligent, and not cheated by the new master, he might accumulate enough money to buy land. It comes as no surprise that few indentured servants later became prominent leaders in seventeenth-century America. The system worked well in that it provided a labor force in a land short of manpower. That is the most that can be said for it.

The Slave

A question that has long divided students of slavery—did the early white settlers bring with them an ingrained prejudice against blacks, or did their prejudice arise out of the humiliating conditions of the blacks' subjection?—seems now to have been answered. The records show "with disturbing clarity," Alden Vaughan has concluded, "that the black men and women brought to Virginia from 1619 to 1629 held from the outset a singularly debased status in the eyes of white Virginians." He agrees with two notable scholars of slavery, Winthrop Jordan and Carl Degler, "that a deep and pervading racial prejudice served as an early and inevitable precursor to American Negro slavery."

But settlement of one question only raises another. As Degler has noted, there is a distinction between prejudice (an attitude) and discrimination (an action). Did the early settlers discriminate from the beginning against the blacks? Edmund Morgan thinks not. "While racial feelings undoubtedly affected the position of Negroes," he writes, "there is more than a little evidence that Virginians during these years were ready to think of Negroes as members or potential members of the community on the same terms as other men and to demand of them the same standards of behavior." T. H. Breen and Stephen Innes have amplified this conclusion in a study of a neighborhood of free blacks on the Eastern Shore of Virginia. They found that in cases of "bastard bearing," black and white fathers were treated equally before the law; each was expected to bear the cost of rearing the child. Free blacks often initiated legal proceedings against white neighbors, and "on the whole their record before the court seems neither better nor worse than that

compiled by small white planters." The courts "showed no re-
luctance to accept the testimony of black planters in cases in-
volving white plaintiffs or defendants." Peter H. Wood found
little discrimination in early South Carolina. "Common hardships and the continuing shortage of hands," he writes, "put the
different races, as well as separate sexes, upon a more equal
footing than they would see in subsequent generations." Many
scholars now conclude that discrimination set in only during the
last quarter of the century when a "series of court decisions and
statutes began closing the gates of freedom along racial lines,"
changes that finally became codified in Virginia's slave code of
1705.

The line between prejudice and discrimination can be fine.
Early settlers judged blacks inferior, and most accepted their
enslavement as natural. A New England visitor in 1687, astonished at the number of blacks he saw, said "there is not a house
in Boston, however small may be its name, that has not one or
two." New York held a large contingent—many, however, free,
for the Dutch seem to have been less prejudiced or more
relaxed about dark-skinned people in their midst—that
amounted to 12 percent of the population. Even in the Delaware Valley Quaker settlers, fervent believers that all men
were created equal, accepted slavery. Yet throughout the
North, blacks seem to have been treated within the family and
before the law much as white indentured servants, which perhaps says no more than that they were not discriminated
against in everyday life because of their color, except, of course,
in their terms of bondage.

Much the same held true in the South during the first three
quarters of the century. There, too, the growth of slavery came
slowly, perhaps for ideological reasons—let not the superior
white culture be debased by the presence of pagan blacks—but
also for practical considerations. First, England had no legal
tradition regarding slavery, which left the settlers with no

guidelines when they bought an enchained black person. Many viewed the black as an indentured servant and used a modified indenture—no terminal date included—to seal the purchase. But questions arose: when a black mated, sometimes with a white woman, what was the status of the child? No one knew. These and scores of other questions helped to slow the growth of slavery. Second, the high death rate during the early years of Chesapeake settlement deterred its growth. Planters found it less risky to buy an indentured servant's labor for a few years than to gamble a lifetime investment in a black who might die within a few months after purchase. Finally, few slavers stopped by the Chesapeake; there were more lucrative markets in the West Indies and Brazil. As a result, slavery took root slowly in the South. The first shipment of blacks, some twenty, arrived in Virginia in 1619. Thirty years later no more than 500 lived in the colony. In 1670, Governor Berkeley counted 2,000 but Wesley Frank Craven thinks this an exaggeration. He agrees, however, that a decade later Virginia had some 3,000 blacks and that by the end of the century a number "somewhat larger but not greatly in excess of 6,000."

The sudden increase, and with it the onset of discrimination, came during the 1670s, and for a number of reasons. Life expectancy in the South had lengthened, thus the risk of buying a black for life lessened; chances now were he would live to repay the original investment. Indentured servants, coupled with the free but poor ex-indentured, had become a disruptive force in the Chesapeake. Slavers, particularly those of the English-chartered Royal African Company, began to pay attention to a bypassed market. Finally, traditions had evolved during the previous half century that clarified the black man's role in society, many of these picked up from settlers of South Carolina who brought from Barbados customs they quickly embodied into a rigid slave code. By the end of the century, for instance, all the South knew that a black man was not only a slave to death but that his offspring must endure the father's bondage; white blood in a child's veins made no difference if mixed to the smallest degree with black. Also, the South had by now eased its mind by creating a stereotype of the blacks. William Fitzhugh, a preeminent Chesapeake planter, in 1686 owned twenty-nine slaves, most of them American-born. He regarded them as draft animals. They "increase," he told a friend, "being all young and a considerable parcel of breeders." A "dumb Negro" he had bought for £23 10s., "bad at work and worse at talking," was something to be rid of, like a lame horse.

The number of blacks in the South rose after the 1670s from 6 to 21 percent of the population, an influx concentrated in Maryland, Virginia, and above all in South Carolina, which in 1700 counted 43 percent of its people black. By that year over 80 percent of blacks in America lived in the South. Meanwhile, their numbers in the North remained fairly static—perhaps 7 percent of the population. Why? Certainly not for economic, social, or even moral reasons, for prejudice was as strong there as elsewhere. Then why? One explanation, perhaps superficial, is that white servants, with all the prejudice of their masters, refused to live in a land where depressed blacks did the work they did. "There is little or no encouragement for men of any tolerable parts to come hither," Virginia's Governor Nicholson said in 1701. He meant that good land and rich widows had become scarce. He also knew that with hoe in hand white servants refused to be equated with blacks. Word spread back to England, and after the 1670s new arrivals generally came to the North, to the Middle Colonies or New England, which throughout the century seldom lacked servants. The more alert among the indentured servants after 1675 or so left the South for colonies where land was more available and where there were fewer blacks.

Meanwhile, the blacks endured. They had been rounded up from everywhere—the New Netherlands, the West Indies, and toward the end of the century directly from Africa. Slavers took care to collect them from various tribes that could not communicate with one another, thus reducing the chance of an uprising aboard ship. Once landed in America, they shared nothing in common except their blackness and enslavement. They were as much at a loss to communicate as the Pennsylvania Dutchman who sought to talk to a Quaker. But their blackness, like the skin of the Indian, made all of them seem the same, and so they were treated. The result was the first true "melting pot" in American history.

"Melting pot" is a myth America cherishes. No such thing existed in early America, with the exception of the blacks. Until well into the twentieth century Jews married only Jews, Protestants only Protestants, and Catholics, Catholics. The same held true for other ethnic groups. Only blacks were forced to meld their origins, traditions, and languages into a single American pot. Overnight, as a historian would say, they had to homogenize themselves into a totally new world. But when the black bent, the white resisted, leaving the black man "suspended between two cultures and able to participate in neither." He was forced to give his labor and he was allowed to give his jigs and variations of his songs to the whites, but they would accept little more. Eventually, the whites opened Christianity to him, but the emphasis went to the Old Testament, where slavery was tolerated, and not to the New Testament, where the word read that all men were created equal.

Only a wisp of uneasiness appeared in early America about the enslavement of blacks. A group of German Quakers spoke out in 1688 for "liberty of body" as well as liberty of conscience, but their plea died on the wind. Samuel Sewall at the end of the century condemned slavery in *The Selling of Joseph*. "Liberty is in real value next unto life," Sewall said. "None ought to part with it themselves, or deprive others of it but upon most mature consideration." But Sewall and a few others cried out alone in the wilderness. Cotton Mather spoke for the multitude. "There is a fondness for freedom in many of you," he told blacks gathered for one of his lectures, and then went on to warn them to live patiently in their servitude, for that was "what God will have . . . appointed to you."

10

A New Kind of Enemy

MOST of the early settlers came to America aware that war in some form might play a large role in their everyday lives, and so it did. Indians met the first contingent to Virginia with the zing of arrows, and their harassment, which twice almost wiped out the colony, continued for a quarter of a century. An early visitor to Plymouth, a settlement relatively untroubled by natives, saw the men march to Sunday meeting carrying muskets that they kept beside them through the service. The musket to the seventeenth-century American became as central to his daily life as the hoe.

The early settlements enlisted professional military officers—notably Captain John Smith (Virginia) and Captain Myles Standish (Plymouth)—but much of their experience meant little in America. Europe fought wars with small, trained armies restrained by strict rules. Sneak attacks and other ungentlemanly maneuvers were unacceptable. Battles were formal set pieces conducted like a game of chess. Two armies lined up on an open field opposite one another, almost close enough to see the whites of the enemy's eyes, for the musket's accuracy did not

extend much beyond fifty yards. The musketeers on order un-
loosed a barrage, and while they slowly reloaded, the cavalry,
equipped with swords and sabers, might then move forward.
Pikesmen stood ready to repel them. The battle ended when
one army withdrew from the field. Civilians were seldom directly involved in all this, and no army sought to exterminate
them as it marched through enemy territory.

All this changed in America. The Indian fought by a different
rule book. He had no use for the formal battle but preferred
isolated skirmishes in which he picked away at the white man
from behind rocks and trees. A Jamestown settler who slipped
from the fort "to do natural necessity" never returned. The
Indian was treacherous. A squad of thirty settler-soldiers lured
into an Indian village never returned. The early Chesapeake
settlers dared neither fish nor hunt nor farm except in armed
groups. "There were never Englishmen left in a foreign country in such misery as we were in this discovered Virginia," said
Smith. Not only did the Indians fight like "unkennell'd wolves,"
but they fought with a terrifying purpose—to push the white
man back into the sea.

The ideally equipped settler-soldier, Smith said, should bring
with him

    1 complete suit of light armor
    1 smoothbore musket five and a half feet long
    1 sword
    1 belt to carry sidearms
    1 bandolier or cartridge belt
    20 pounds of powder
    60 pounds of shot

Few of the early settlers came thus equipped. A large majority
had never held a musket in their hands. Most were useless as
soldiers, "being for the most part of such tender educations and
small experience in martial accidents." The few who arrived

outfitted as Smith wished presented an imposing appearance but hardly one adequate for wilderness warfare. Weighted down as they were, they moved slowly against a nimble enemy. The Indian carried only a quiver of arrows and a light bow. In the time it took the white man to shoulder his awkward musket, fire once, then reload, the Indian could send off from six to ten arrows. The arrow was less damaging than the soft-lead shot from a musket (when it found its target), but it could stop a man, and was more accurate over a longer distance. The Indian had the advantage, if he had only known it. If he could have overcome his awe of the booming gun and put aside tribal rivalries —an impossibility, of course, given the lengthy history and intensity of those rivalries—long enough to present a united front, the white man might easily have been pushed back into the sea. As it was, the Indian nearly succeeded in doing so several times through the seventeenth century.

Before the earliest attempts to settle America, England had been forced to amend the ritual form of warfare when it invaded Ireland during Elizabeth I's reign. There it faced a wild, uncivilized country filled with belligerent natives who also fought by their own rules. Like the Indians, they favored guerrilla warfare. The English reacted by establishing military beachheads in a hostile land, building garrisons ringed by stout palisades. (For soldiers to go beyond the "pale" meant to risk death.) Neither Smith nor Standish had fought in Ireland, but they must have heard enough from veterans of campaigns there to see that circumstances in America were similar. Both men dealt competently with a novel situation, but Smith, who faced more formidable opposition from the natives and left an abundant record of how he dealt with it, deserves the fuller attention he has received.

After Smith took command of Jamestown through force of will, personality, and initiative, he had the fort rebuilt. He posted sentries to patrol the ramparts around the clock. He inaugurated drills every Saturday morning on a field in the shadow of the fort (eventually called Smithfield), "where sometimes more than an hundred savages would stand in amazement to behold how a file would batter a tree, where [Smith] would make them a mark to shoot at." When food ran short, he took the best of his company and marched or sailed into Indian country and forced tribes to contribute to the white man's welfare. He had run the operation for only a year when a nearly fatal wound forced him to return home and by "ill chance to end when he had but only learned how to begin." But he left behind a hundred "well trained and expert soldiers," a stout fort defended by twenty-four cannons, three hundred firearms, a stockpile of pikes, swords, and helmets. His advice helped convince the London Company's management in 1610 to send out a new contingent of settlers led by "excellent old soldiers," many of whom had served in Ireland, "that university of war." For a number of years thereafter Virginia resembled a military encampment overseas. The governor, though a civilian, was commander in chief of the armed forces, and most of his council bore military titles. Settlers were organized under captains and ruled by martial law. English liberties were for the time being allowed to lapse.

Virginia relaxed martial law and revived accustomed liberties when the Indian menace seemed to abate. But a basic problem remained there as elsewhere in America. Throughout most of the seventeenth century the Crown refused to give substantial military aid to any colony; that cost money which it refused to spend. The London Company assumed much of the burden in Virginia as did the Dutch West India Company in New Netherlands, but in both instances the expense proved prohibitive. A better solution to a unique problem had to be produced quickly if the frail colonies were to survive. The settlers found it, or thought they had, in an institution they had known at home—the militia.

The Militia

In Anglo-Saxon times all able-bodied men were inducted into the fryd, a local organization designed to defend the shire or county from intruders. By the seventeenth century the fryd had been transmuted into the militia, which was still concerned with military defense on the local scene but was otherwise quite different. Hardly more than a tenth of the men of a county belonged to the militia. It had become a social as much as a military organization, composed mainly of the county's substantial men. Only the fairly well off could afford the musket, ball and shot, the pike, sword, or other military paraphernalia with which each member must equip himself. Cost, as well as the Crown's eagerness to keep the often restless lower classes unarmed, prevented most men from joining. The militia mustered once or twice a year. Citizens from all parts of the county gathered to watch the troops perform their drills and perhaps engage in a sham battle; the rest of the day was given over to drinking and other pleasures. The militia played no part in the conduct of war. England's isolation gave little cause to fear invasion, and by Cromwell's time in the 1640s the militia had become mainly a police force to put down riots and other internal disturbances.

As in so many instances, the settlers kept the name and form of an old institution but otherwise changed it radically. The militia in America still drew its members from the local community—the town in New England, the county elsewhere. Members were still obliged to equip themselves. Officers, whether elected as in New England (a practice later abrogated) or appointed as in the Chesapeake, usually came from the gentry. Muster days, as complaining ministers observed every year, continued to resemble a carnival. With these relics of the past, resemblance to the English model ended. The American version no longer comprised only the upper classes. All able-bodied men from sixteen to sixty were required to serve. Behind the new assumption that all men had a duty to protect their community lay another that also broke with English tradition—all men had the right to bear arms. (This was not, however, entirely a break with English tradition; it owed much to civic traditions, as J. G. A. Pocock has pointed out.) Fear of the Indians outweighed fear of internal revolt.

Europeans, judging by what they saw on muster days, had only disdain for the American militia. "There was a training and muster today," said a visitor to New York in 1680. "Some were on horseback, and six small companies were on foot. They were exercised in military tactics, but I have never seen anything worse of the kind." Some years later another laughed at the "diversity of weapons and dresses, unsizeableness of the men, and want of the least grain of discipline in their officers or them" as he viewed a muster day in Virginia. Typically, these days began with a morning of drilling, followed by footraces and other sporting events, and ending, at least for one Virginia muster, with a hogshead of punch being rolled out, which "entertained all the people and made them drunk and fighting all the evening, but without mischief." No wonder Europeans derided what they saw of the militia.

Yet they should have sensed that everyone regarded muster days as holidays and judged them as such. They should have also realized that the men they watched stumbling across a marching field were a ragtag collection of civilians who through the year gathered only occasionally as a unit and spent the rest of their time with a hoe in hand. They were not culled from the population, like the Coldstream Guard, which accepted only men at least six feet tall, trained them through the year, then put them on display, uniforms and equipment glistening, feet dropping as one as they marched along, to fill the public with awe. The question visitors should have asked—none did—was how by comparison to their European counterparts did the American militia perform in the field? Only an equivocal answer can be given. First, the quality of performance depended, as always, on the quality of the leaders, which up and down the coast varied from superb to deplorable. Second, seldom did a commander mobilize all the men a visitor saw fumbling through a muster day. When a crisis arose, he selected the stout and sturdy, the intrepid, and his best marksmen to move into the field. If he chose well, the men performed admirably. Regardless of European derision, the American militia was an adequate solution, for a time, to an American dilemma: How could a people unable to support a standing army defend itself against an omnipresent enemy that fought war by its own rules? The solution had flaws that emerged as the century wore on.

Adjustments

The early settlers saw at once that war in America would not be what it had been in Europe. They quickly learned to fight the Indian by his own rules. "God pleased to show us the vanity of our military skill in managing our arms after the European mode," a New Englander said. "Now we are glad to learn the skulking way of war," and, he added (as if ashamed to have sunk to the Indian's level), "what God's end is in teaching us such a way of discipline I know not." They soon saw that the close-order drill practiced on muster days was a useless tactic against Indian warriors. "It is one thing to drill a company in a plain champaign and another to drive an enemy through desert woods," said a contemporary. Instead, they marched through the forest "at a wide distance from one another, . . . [as] this was an Indian custom to march thin and scatter." It became customary to put out scouts on the flanks to anticipate a surprise attack. Unnecessary talk was discouraged and smoking forbidden. At the first sign of attack the leader shouted "Tree all!" and all dove for cover.

The whites adopted the Indian strategy of total war. John Endecott of Massachusetts Bay wiped out entire villages during the Pequot War of 1637. Those who survived were enslaved and exported to the West Indies. In King Philip's War of 1675–76, the Indians raped, scalped, and skinned their captives and burned villages to the ground. It was not uncommon for a soldier to come upon a murdered pregnant woman with the embryo ripped from her womb and "elevated on a stick or pole, as a trophy of victory and an object of horror to the survivors of the slain." The whites retaliated with similar brutality. After King Philip had been killed, the troops cut off his head and hands, quartered his body, and hung the parts on trees. James Axtell reports on an incident during the war when a commander ordered an Indian woman "to be torn to pieces by dogs." Two years later in Marblehead, Massachusetts, "a group of women emerging from church set upon two Indian prisoners from Maine and with their bare hands literally tore them apart. An eyewitness reported that 'we found [the Indians] with their heads off and gone, and their flesh in a manner pulled from their bones.' "

(English brutality, it should be noted, was not simply a reaction to Indian barbarism. The early settlers, Puritans included, had emerged out of the lusty, ruthless Elizabethan age. Captain John Smith's history of Virginia—really his autobiography—is a tale of blood and violence told by a man who counted Cortez among his heroes of the past and among his contemporaries such swaggering, boastful, merciless gentlemen as Sir Walter Raleigh and Sir Francis Drake. Brutality toward non-English opponents—notably the Irish and Scots—and even with their own, as in the Puritan Revolution, was a quality of seventeenth-century life that England passed on to America.)

As tactics and strategy changed, so too did equipment. According to Axtell, most of the accoutrements common in the British army—"the long pikes, heavy matchlocks with rests, carriage cannon, brightly colored uniforms, ponderous supply trains, and female camp followers"—vanished. A lighter, shorter musket, easier to carry through the forest, came into general use. The barrel was coated brown to prevent glinting. The men wore moccasins—"without Indian shoes, they can't perform their duty"—and carried backpacks that were small and light, some thirty pounds lighter than those hoisted by a British soldier; they held blankets, field provisions, and perhaps an extra pair or two of moccasins. Body armor remained in use for many years, although worn mainly by officers who could afford it and who used it as much as a status symbol as for protection. Heavily padded coats and jackets replaced armor, and the men wore outfits that blended into the forest background, either buckskins or shirts and breeches dyed dark green. Expensive, awkward swords and sabers gave way to axes, hatchets, tomahawks, and scalping knives. Pikes were reserved for public drills and ceremonial parades.

Only in times of extreme danger did the militia resemble what it appeared to be on paper—a vehicle for universal military training. Almost anyone eager to avoid service could find a way. The well-to-do might escape by paying a fine or hiring a substitute. Exemptions varied from colony to colony, but in a list compiled by Douglas Leach they included such public officials as magistrates and judges, clerks of the court, sheriffs and constables. Also exempted were physicians and surgeons, ministers and deacons, schoolmasters and students, millers and mariners. Craftsmen crucial to a colony's economy, such as miners and furnace workers in an embryonic iron industry, were not required to serve. As the century wore on and a body of discontented blacks and whites arose in the South, leaders there denied them the right to bear arms or serve in the militia—blacks in Virginia in 1639 and indentured servants a number of years later. Eventually in all colonies those who served on active duty were the young, free whites. The slaughter of a band of New England militiamen did not lead to a lament for the loss of a spectrum from the male population but to the "ruin of a choice company of young men, the very flower of the county."

The militia system had other flaws. It invariably failed to anticipate surprise attacks, the Indians' favorite and most successful weapon. It was not, as William Shea remarks, "a force in being, but a segment of the population to be mobilized in response to an immediate and specific threat or the actual outbreak of hostilities." Once alerted it could react swiftly—Massachusetts Bay put twelve hundred men in the field within an hour or so after Indians raided a town thirty miles inland—but in the field other weaknesses developed. No colony during the century developed an informed, forceful central command to direct operations over its various self-centered companies, nor did any produce experienced quartermasters to keep troops on the march supplied. Intercolonial cooperation materialized rarely. Massachusetts in 1691 refused to join New York in a joint assault on Canada, though French direction of Indian raids on both colonies was obvious to all. Rhode Island and Connecticut, in turn, later refused to aid an oppressed Massachusetts.

The effectiveness of the militia was tied to the imminence of danger. Early Virginia ordered every Sunday a training day, with all males required to bring a musket to church and drill after service. A decade later muster days were reduced to once a month. After an Indian onslaught in 1622 that nearly demolished the colony yet left enough settlers alive to reply with a murderous offensive, a complacency set in that led them to neglect "to stand upon their guard or to keep their arms fit and ready about them." The colony survived another stupendous Indian attack in 1644—the last the Chesapeake had to endure —and in the relaxed atmosphere that followed, musters were reduced to three times a year. As the Indian menace waned, the militia became mainly a social organization. A third of the Massachusetts legislature tacked military titles onto their names to indicate their status, and in Virginia's House of Burgesses the proportion ran higher. An early-eighteenth-century visitor remarked that wherever one went in the South "your ears are constantly astonished at the number of colonels, majors, and captains that you hear mentioned. In short, the whole country seems at first to you a retreat for heroes."

On paper the militia fostered an illusion that the colonies had a well-trained and armed civilian population that could defend itself against any enemy. Most colonial leaders by midcentury knew the facts were otherwise and sought alternatives. The Dutch of New Netherlands, with no militia tradition to fall back on, relied chiefly on negotiations and diplomacy in dealing with the powerful Iroquois Confederacy. Late-settled Pennsylvania, dominated by pacifist Quakers who deplored militias, adopted a similar technique, which worked well until the Indians in the expanding neighborhood became a menace in the eighteenth century. New England experimented with garrisons, sturdy houses scattered along the frontier, to which families could flee in a time of troubles. Governor Berkeley of Virginia wanted a force of five hundred professional soldiers in the colony's pay, but settlers balked at the expense. Instead, he tried to create a buffer between red and white by building a string of block-houses along the frontier, manned by militiamen on short tours of duty. Leaders in both the North and South also conceived of isolated reservations for the Indian from which the white man was to be excluded. Various imaginative approaches to a unique problem were tried, but all failed under the steady encroachment of the white man into the interior.

Nothing on earth—no garrison or blockhouse, no militia, not even a group of trained mercenaries—could reassure the inland settler except his gun, and even that did not always give dependable protection. One reason so many choice flowers died in the field is that many of them went out with flawed weapons. Even the relatively simple musket often needed repairs, and a locksmith who specialized in such work could seldom be found except in port towns that gave him enough trade to keep busy throughout the year. His craft called for considerable skill and training, and also a large outlay in stock. Robert F. Trent has printed the inventory of one who died in Boston in 1668. In addition to 212 pounds of iron, no minor investment, his shop held over a hundred various tools and pieces of equipment, among them some twenty different chisels, screw plates to make screws, a stock drill, a "block to unbreech guns," and a "windless on the block to pull the barrel of the gun free of a broken stock." The chances were fifty-fifty that without such a shop at hand a militiaman might carry to muster day and even into battle a musket that needed some kind of repair. And even if his weapon were in perfect shape, a shower of rain left him defenseless, for a musket would not fire in wet weather. Thus ill-prepared were the settlers for the string of French and Indian Wars that began in 1690 and lasted well into the eighteenth century.

11

WOOD AND WATER · TRAVEL · THE MEETINGHOUSE · PORT TOWNS

Wood and Water

No MAN in seventeenth-century America could have written the lines "I think that I shall never see/A poem lovely as a tree." Trees were obstacles that had to be cleared away. They were also a commodity that could be converted into fuel, useful artifacts, and above all money. Wood was America's chief natural resource, central to the everyday life of all settlers, and all used it with abandon. When wood became scarce in the vicinity of a farm, it gave a man reason to think about moving on. Oxen proliferated in early America as much to haul timber from the forest as to pull plows. Few craftsmen could survive without wood. To smelt a ton of iron required some 140 bushels of charcoal drawn from five cords of wood. It took a cord to convert seawater into eleven bushels of salt. A householder with two fireplaces needed over thirty cords to carry him through the year. It horrified visitors to view Americans' profligate use of what remained a precious commodity at home.

Profligate, yes, but also selective. Within a generation settlers learned to distinguish the virtues of various trees. Coopers found the white oak superior for wine barrels, shipbuilders preferred it for topside planking, carpenters for house frames. Black oak's resistance to tropical worms made it ideal for the underwater part of a ship's hull. Red oak worked well for sugar and molasses barrels and for wainscoting within a house. Hickory produced the best and hottest fire. Chestnut and cedar were favored for fence posts because they resisted rotting. Cedar had a further virtue—its lightness made it ideal for shingles and clapboard siding. Tanners preferred the bark of sumacs, chestnuts, willows, and especially oaks. Soapmakers were not particular; any cartload of ashes suited their needs. Coopers bound the staves for their barrels, pails, tubs, buckets, and churns with hoops made from withy, pliable willow branches. Carpenters liked white pine for flooring in houses. New England entrepreneurs developed the most profitable market for trees. In New Hampshire and Maine a tree often soared to over a hundred feet, a perfect ship's mast when stripped of branches. Hitherto England's navy and merchant marine had depended on imports from Scandinavia of pines usually so short they had to be spliced to make a single mast. America offered relief from this dependence, and by 1670 Portsmouth, New Hampshire, alone was sending ten shiploads a year of white-pine masts to the mother country.

A mast could be shipped much as it came from the forest, but a house or a ship called for planks and boards. The settlers brought from home two techniques to convert logs into lumber. One was to rive the log with wedge and ax, a process that took considerable skill. The other was to saw it by hand. Sawyers laid the log over a pit about twelve feet long and five feet deep. With one man below, the other above, they used a long, two-handled ripsaw to transform the log into lumber. (Excessive drinking prevailed among sawyers, and they took numerous breaks during the day to refresh themselves; though they regularly changed positions, the man below needed respites from the blizzard of sawdust that rained down.) Both techniques persisted throughout the century, but a third—the sawmill—quickly supplemented them. Two sawyers could turn out about a hundred board feet a day; a sawmill could produce that amount in an hour or less.

At this point water and wood came together. America had innumerable fast-running streams to power a sawmill's water-wheel, but it lacked expertise to build the wheel or construct the mill, for England at the time, and for decades thereafter, had no sawmills. Driven by local needs for massive amounts of lumber and by an awareness of ready markets in England and the West Indies eager to buy all they could produce, the settlers accepted the sawmill with alacrity. Within four years after the first ships arrived in the Chesapeake one was erected on the James River, built by German craftsmen especially imported for the work. The Dutch, accustomed to wind-driven mills, put one up soon after settling New Amsterdam. Four years after the settlement of Massachusetts Bay a sawmill appeared there, this time built by Danish experts. The success of tobacco as a cash crop coupled with the lazy flowing rivers that emptied into the Chesapeake inhibited the spread of sawmills there, but in the North they proliferated. By 1700 nearly every town in New England that lay along a stream had a sawmill. Along the barely settled Maine–New Hampshire coast some sixty sawmills were turning out hundreds of thousands of boards and planks annually.

The sawmill built early America, but the farmer who brought logs to it was only vaguely aware how it affected not only his own everyday life but the everyday life of those beyond his horizon. Once his logs reached the mill—he could float soft-woods downstream, but hardwoods had to be hauled overland by oxen—and he collected that due to him, his mind turned back to the farm. European visitors, on the other hand, were appalled by the waste the American sawmill produced. A fifth of every log ended up as sawdust, compared to less than an eighth wasted by sawyers using a thin ripsaw blade. Worse, mill owners handled the sawdust cavalierly. Some shoveled the debris into a neighboring marsh or swamp, but most dumped it into the stream that turned the waterwheel, making once clear water turbid. The polluted streams soon drove fish away, and where once Indians and whites had harvested tons of herring, salmon, and other fish that came back each spring to spawn, now there were none.

No one of that day gave thought to waste or pollution, because early America wanted lumber. The port towns could not have survived without sawmills. Shipyards and housing booms created an insatiable demand for boards and planks that had to be satisfied. Most mills were small operations, run by one or two men but owned by merchants in the port towns. Mills cost money to erect and only the merchants had the money to risk. The up-and-down steel-edged saw had to be imported from Europe, along with the iron accoutrements that kept it running. A skilled mason had to be found to put together the mill's stone foundation. A carpenter trained to construct waterwheels had to be enticed to the construction site. The retaining dam and sluice often needed to assure a steady supply of water to turn the wheel had to be built. Even after the mill began operation, the risks remained high. An iced-over stream could close it down in winter, the easiest time to haul logs from the forest. A spring freshet might wash out the retaining dam and wreck the waterwheel. A summer drought often kept the machinery idle.

All the risks involved in operating a sawmill were duplicated in a gristmill, but there comparison ended. A gristmill called for a much larger capital investment—no other colonial enterprise except shipbuilding required more—mainly because the stones needed to grind grain had to be imported from Europe. Once the stones reached a port town they had to be hauled inland—another heavy expense—and then assembled and dressed at the mill site by an expert. Grist milling, compared to mechanical sawing, was a highly specialized craft. The ideal miller combined the skills of carpenter, cooper, joiner, blacksmith, and mason. He needed to be able to judge with eye and hand the quality of the grain, its age, its moisture content, its temperature, and then determine the proper speed to rotate his stones for the particular batch in hand.

Every community that fronted on a fast-running stream did all it could to lure a miller into its midst. In addition to the mill site it often gave him a choice plot of land. Invariably it promised him a monopoly and a royalty or toll that varied from 10 to 15 percent on every bushel ground into flour. An English saying had it that "no miller goes to heaven," and children were taught that when they found a miller with a tuft of hair growing from his palm they had come upon an honest miller. Given this traditional suspicion, most communities tried to impose restraints on the miller. His monopoly generally had a time limit on it which might not be renewed if his performance failed to satisfy the neighborhood. A contract usually restricted charges to customers. The gristmill, in short, was treated as a public utility. The aim was "to adjust private enterprise to community ends."

Others in the community might have more prestige, but no one exceeded the miller in practical importance. His presence could mean the difference between a subsistence existence and prosperity. Without him all grain had to be ground by hand and few farmers could produce enough surplus flour by that process to send to market. Flour the miller shipped to port towns returned in the form of pots and pans, axes and hoes, bolts of calico. Some millers opened small stores to serve the neighborhood. Often a hamlet cropped up around the mill site as it slowly became the economic and social center of the area. By the end of the century the gristmill and to a lesser extent the sawmill, both powered by water, worked for the backcountry of early America as an "entering wedge of a slowly emerging market economy." Both served the isolated settler as a window on the world beyond the farm.

Travel

The average Englishman did little traveling. Everything he wanted—the church, the pub, the blacksmith, even the land he farmed—lay close by in easy walking distance. All was different in America. Travel was a part of everyday life. A trip to church or meeting, to a wedding, to the muster field or the gristmill might vary from five to fifteen miles, even farther. Driving a herd of cattle to market could entail a trek of fifty miles. Most settlers did not venture beyond their colonial borders, but within those borders they were constantly on the move by land and water.

Most early settlers lived within easy distance of navigable water, either on the seacoast or along some river that served as a liquid highway to take people inland and their surplus produce downstream to a port town. As Braudel remarks, "water brought animation to the land all around." One of the few constants in American history has been the continuing cheapness of water transportation. In 1834 a ton of goods shipped from Europe to an American port three thousand miles away could be moved inland at the same cost only thirty miles. That statistic without undue warping can be read back into the seventeenth century, when roads were no more than ruts in the land. But travel by water for the average settler had drawbacks. As a rule he lacked the talent to build anything more sophisticated than a dugout canoe. Even if he had the skill to build a boat, he probably lacked the money to buy an iron anchor or the lines and canvas needed for sails. Finally, for the landlubber sailing could be dangerous; without warning, nature could inflict on the innocent such things as squalls, thunderstorms, fogs, and tides that left him helpless. Even in the "well-watered" Chesapeake region, where a boat would have seemed a necessity, one scholar has found that such craft "do not loom large in seventeenth century inventories until the 1680s, when about

22.5 percent of the estates possessed them." Freight traffic on water moved in boats built by craftsmen and piloted by experienced sailors. Plain people paddled their canoes to cross rivers, visit neighbors, and to fish; otherwise they traveled by land.

Despite the myriad waterways, most of America moved about by land, usually on horseback from midcentury on. By the early 1680s some 80 percent of the farmers in the Chesapeake, a land supposedly addicted to water travel, owned at least one horse. An overland trip was safe compared to one in England, where robberies were a common fear. It was inexpensive; the horses fed themselves, and lonely farm families along the way usually welcomed a traveler's company, feeding and putting him and his horse up for the night just to hear him talk about the outside world. It was also speedy by standards of the day. The small but sturdy bay horse, popular throughout the colonies, was known as the "everlaster." "Our horses in this country go so easy that a ride of fifty miles, perhaps, won't tire a man as much as twenty or thirty miles with your horses in England," said one man. "They make nothing of traveling sixty miles a day, which few horses in England can perform."

Travel by land had drawbacks—squalid inns if no welcoming farmer could be found for the night, ferries that ran at their owners' whims and charged high. Often a path ran through a farmer's property, which meant constant dismounting to open and shut gates. Worst of all, there were no road signs. The paths were designed for local use; everyone in the neighborhood knew where they led, but strangers inevitably got lost, even when someone had taken time to blaze the trail. "These marks," said one distraught traveler, "are merely a piece cut out of the bark with an ax, about the height of a man's eyes from the ground; and by means of them the commonest roads are designated through all New Netherland and Maryland; but in consequence of the great number of roads so marked, and their running into and across each other, they are of little assistance, and indeed often mislead." The traveler goes on to recount a not untypical day in the Chesapeake.

> We missed the road, although we were upon it, and could not find that or any other plantation, and meanwhile it became dark. . . . We were utterly perplexed and astray. We followed the roads as we found them, now easterly and then westerly, now a little more on one side, and then a little more on the other, until we were completely tired out, and wished ourselves back again upon the strand. We had to keep on however, or remain in the woods, and as the latter did not suit us, we chose the former, fatigued as we were, and uncertain as was the issue. I plucked up courage and went singing along, which resounded through the woods, although I was short of breath through weariness.

Nine o'clock that night the party heard a dog barking. They whacked a path through bushes to a farmhouse. "We were strangers here, and had no address to these people, who, nevertheless showed us every kindness and treated us well. . . . They told us we had lost the way at the empty house, by taking the road to the left instead of the right."

The Meetinghouse

The church, regardless of a family's religious or ethnic background, gave the most intimate, lasting tie beyond the farm. To call it a church, however, misleads. The New England term *meetinghouse* serves better, for it was the single place for country people where almost everyone met more or less regularly. Men went to the gristmill, attended court days, or shared drinks in the tavern, but the entire family traveled to church. The Sabbath offered everyone a break from the deadening routine of everyday life and the chance for all to renew ties with the neighborhood. In a land without newspapers the meetinghouse was the place to gather news and gossip. In a land without theaters a lively minister might, while uplifting the souls of his flock, also broaden their horizons and just possibly in the process entertain them. Finally, there were the hymns in which all could join. In the Chesapeake, which took its religion more lightly than elsewhere, men often conducted business before and after service. If a denomination offered two Sunday services, those who came from a distance and planned to stay for both might pass the time over a picnic dinner. The day called for a serious demeanor, but given the behavior of children through the ages it is likely they found ways to enjoy friends they could see only on the Sabbath.

Most settlers came from communities in Europe where the local church dated back a century or more. They took what the past had handed down to them. Now in America they must start afresh, and though they might know none of their new neighbors their first sense of community in many instances stemmed from the joint effort to build a house of worship. They faced considerable problems. First, where to locate the building. It had to be placed at a spot reasonably accessible to all in the neighborhood—a crossroads, perhaps, in the South, a hamlet or village in the North. How large should it be? That depended on the number of worshippers in the area. Next, someone had to be found who was able to build it. The design varied with demands imposed by the congregation and the talent of the builder, but regardless of the denomination, early American meetinghouses tended to resemble one another. Tradition has it that they were relatively simple structures because of the simple existence in the wilderness and the limited skill of available craftsmen. There is something to this, but the architecture of the early meetinghouses also owed much to the plain style of religious architecture that had been developing in Europe as an answer to the ornateness of Catholic cathedrals. All the ingredients of the early churches—stark interiors, clear windows, two-story facades, blunt towers (steeples came much later)—had been evolving for nearly a century among Protestant builders in England, Holland, Germany, and Huguenot France. American builders invented little in what has since been called a characteristically American religious architecture.

Woven into all these questions was the crucial one of cost. Generally, it was assessed in proportion to a member's ability to pay. Some contributed labor or materials or both. Others paid in cash or produce. Whatever a man's assessment, none could dismiss it lightly. John Coolidge reports that the total cost to build a new meetinghouse for Hingham, Massachusetts, in 1680 was approximately five hundred pounds. This sum, he goes on, was four and a half times the cost of the finest residence and ten times that of an average house, six times the minister's annual salary, and seven times the yearly cost of running the town. The figures are more striking when reduced to the context of a plain farmer's everyday life:

> In 1680 a bushel of oats was worth one shilling and six pence, a bushel of Indian corn two and six, a barrel of cider eight and six. A day's wages for cutting wood was two shillings. At these prices the standard minimum contribution of twenty shillings represented eight bushels of corn. It would have taken an ordinary laborer ten days to earn that much money. Perhaps as a very rough rule of thumb one should consider that a pound in the Hingham of 1680 was worth one hundred and fifty dollars of our money today [1961].

Once a house of worship was up, every community in the land could boast, as did a New Englander, that it had been built "by our own vote, framed by our own hammers and saws, and by our own hands set in the convenientest place for us all." The congregation had created it, paid for it, owned it and the land upon which it rested. They repaired or enhanced it when the need arose. The state had little say in how they conducted their affairs. Control within each church, throughout the colonies, lay with a select group—the vestry, elders, deacons, and the like. Only in the eighteenth century did congregations up and down the land insist that ultimate power within their churches lay with them, not the elite, an explosion that came to be called the Great Awakening.

Port Towns

An awareness of the multitude of footpaths and ways that meandered everywhere in early America should long ago have disillusioned historians about the self-sufficient farm. The traditional picture is a myth. Few farmers knew how to tan leather nor their wives how to convert it into a buckskin suit or moccasins. Few wives spun thread from wool or flax or wove it into cloth, for most farms through three quarters of the century lacked both spinning wheels and looms. The self-sufficient farm rarely, if ever, existed in early America, and everyday life was from the beginning tied to the world beyond the farm. Paths led settlers to other farms, to and from social events, but equally to spots where they exchanged goods. In the Chesapeake this might be to the site of a well-to-do planter who had acquired enough capital to outfit a small store; in the North to a hamlet, village, or a port town where a cow or horse, a barrel of apples or flour could be bartered into a pan, powder and shot, or a length of cloth. From the beginning trade permeated the everyday life of every farmer. Trade, said a contemporary, "animates the farmer, keeps him to his plough, brightens and enlivens all his rural schemes, reconciles him to all his hard labor, and makes him look fat and cheerful."

Most of this was petty trade, even when it led to port towns. Uncle Ben Hosmer, a farmer from Concord, Massachusetts, decided "one dog-day morning in August" to go to market in Cambridge. He had run out of rum and that helped to impel him toward town. He had neither a wagon nor an ox to pull it, and so he slung parcels of his wife's eggs and butter over the back of his old mare. The upshot of the trip is inconsequential to all save Uncle Ben, and for his sake let it be concluded: If all had gone well he would have returned with a jug of rum and perhaps something for the wife. Instead, along the way Uncle Ben relented at the sight of his lathered horse and paused to let her drink. The mare had more in mind—a cool bath, to be specific—and rolled in the stream. "Don't you know any better than to lie down in the brook with Dinah's butter and egg on your condemned back?" Uncle Ben raved as he watched a vision of rum vanish downstream in egg yolks.

Uncle Ben's aborted trip occurred in the 1790s, but the trivial merchandise he carried typified what a seventeenth-century farmer brought to market. Ship captains in the port towns spent much of their time piecing together cargoes from the spare offerings farmers brought to them. The manifest from one ship headed for the West Indies probably differed little from scores of others that departed from northern ports:

> 5 horses, 56 hogs, 84 geese, 190 hens, 4,460 feet of lumber, 1,900 staves, 5,500 shingles, 11 barrels of fish, 7 barrels of apples, 1,700 pounds of cheese.

Some ships were outfitted with built-in pens to carry only animals, a profitable but exacerbating cargo. "For each horse, cow, ox, or sheep bound for the West Indies," Howard Russell reports, "a vessel had to take aboard 200 to 500 pounds of hay according to destination; for each horse, 10 to 15 bushels of oats also. A ship loading 50 horses might need as much as 10 to 12 tons of pressed hay and 500 more bushels of oats in addition to food for the crew."

The port towns have been called "cities in the wilderness," but in the seventeenth century none, even Boston, amounted to more than towns. Yet where they flourished, which was everywhere except in the Chesapeake, they were what "the heart is to the human body in circulating the blood." They drew in from the hinterland lumber, produce, and livestock, used some of it for themselves and sent the surplus on to other colonies or abroad in ships they had built. Every port town had a

shipyard. By the end of the century New England alone had a
fleet of some two thousand vessels, fishing smacks excluded,
most of them built in its own ports. Profits from shipbuilding,
along with those from fishing and merchandizing, led local capi-
talists to invest in sawmills in Maine and elsewhere, in gristmills
along backcountry streams. Craftsmen in the towns transformed the raw material the hinterland sent them. Tanned
hides became leather gloves and jackets. Wheelwrights produced carts, wagons, sometimes even chaises if they had the
skill; coopers combined staves into barrels; carpenters built
wharves and houses; and shipwrights, ropemakers, sailmakers,
and blacksmiths, among others, joined together to create boats
and ships.

In contrast to farmers, the everyday lives of townspeople
differed little from what they had known in England. They
walked to and from work, for every port town clung close to the
waterfront. The church bell resounded in their ears throughout
the week. Market day occurred regularly as it had in England,
and fairs, too, became fixtures on the calendar. Houses were
jammed close together and no one who desired it wanted for
companionship. The hogs that ran wild in the streets evoked no
comment, nor did the stench from accumulated garbage, nor in
summer the tormenting mosquitoes or the clouds of flies that
blackened uncovered food. Townspeople lived their days amid
the noise of clanging hammers, the rumblings of carts and wagons, the squalling of children—all of which sounded like music
after a trip to the country, where only twittering birds relieved
the silence. At night, raucous sailors rolling through town on
shore leave, heading toward local brothels—even puritanical
Boston had its share—were minor irritants to a daily life filled
with tension, perhaps, but also with endless variety.

The ships that brought sailors brought goods that kept port
towns bustling—ironware, pewter, windowpanes, paint, car-
pets, and curtains—but they also carried newspapers, journals,
books, and travelers bursting with gossip. The towns were ori-

ented toward England. Painting, architecture, furniture, the bowl a silversmith made—all were necessarily patterned on English models. If the elite in England wore periwigs, then the fashion prevailed here. When the newfangled fork became *au courant* for dining, then the best in the port towns trained themselves to use it. Close ties with England kept class distinctions alive in the towns as they waned in the countryside. Craftsmen continued, as at home, to wear leather aprons, gentlemen, small clothes—knickers, silk stockings, silk shirts, and, at the end of the century, periwigs—to set themselves apart. Workmen walked, gentlemen traveled in chaises (often imported from abroad), with a black at the reins if they could afford a slave. The farmer who brought cattle or horses, a barrel of apples or onions, even a parcel or two of eggs and butter, to a port town knew the instant he arrived he touched on a world far beyond the farm.

12

WONDERS OF
THE INVISIBLE WORLD

SIGNS AND SUPERSTITIONS · MOON WATCHING · WITCHCRAFT IN SALEM ·
ADDENDUM

Signs and Superstitions

PLAIN PEOPLE and the educated in early America shared a common belief in signs, celestial and otherwise. God revealed Himself through the Scriptures and His power and glory through nature. Often, however, His celestial signs were ambiguous. The sudden flaring of a comet across the sky could be interpreted—as more than one minister did—as "Heaven's Alarm to the World," or as no more than a display of God's boundless power. A brilliant display of northern lights convinced many this was God's forewarning of the world's end; when the end failed to come, men had to ponder further what the sign meant. Unraveling the meaning of celestial occurrences endlessly engrossed the wise and foolish throughout the century. What did God intend to indicate by an eclipse, or by a shower of falling stars?

These and other heavenly displays rarely touched everyday lives directly, except through the moon's pull of the tides. God offered other signs to keep the settlers alert to their sinfulness. John Winthrop found a sinful provocation in every calamity that overtook an individual. Others were equally perceptive.

The disobedience of two unruly servants ordained their drowning. A village swept by fire should have expected the event, for it had failed to provide "an able, faithful dispenser of the word of God." All natural disasters were a sign of God's wrath. The Virginia Indians' onslaught in 1622 stemmed from the "sins of drunkenness and excess of apparel" among the settlers. A blight that ruined New England's wheat crops for a string of years originated in the senseless persecution of Quakers. God punished Massachusetts for its persecuting laws with King Philip's War in 1675. Not all untoward events could be attributed to God. Satan, too, had a role. Who else but he would have struck so many churches with bolts of lightning? Haunted houses were of his doing, and those accused of being witches were clearly his victims.

Everyone could debate the meaning of providential signs, but superstitions carried clear mandates not to be contravened. A black cat crossing one's path was an omen of bad luck, but the same cat's blood had medicinal value; hence in some settlements "there was scarcely a black cat whose ears and tail had not been frequently cropped for a contribution of blood." To break a mirror also assured bad luck in the near future, and for some it forecast an early death in the family. Every ethnic group brought its own set of superstitions from home. The Swedes, for instance, believed that with the sale of a healthy cow the owner must snip a hank of its hair to keep good luck on the farm; that saying the Lord's Prayer backward could prevent rain during a harvest; that though no man dared witness the event, all their cattle on Christmas Eve briefly acquired the power of speech. The Germans held that if New Year's Day fell on Sunday a mild winter and pleasant spring lay ahead and "all manner of good things shall abound"; that anyone born during the first three days of a new year was doomed to an unhappy life; that a newly purchased pig must be backed into the pen to assure it a healthy life. In Virginia a man who stum-

bled over a grave in an abandoned field knew he must jump
backward over it, otherwise a kinsman would soon die. A stranger might regard another man's superstitions with amusement,
but his own were not to be questioned. They were part and
parcel of his everyday life.

Moon Watching

The educated probably took many superstitions lightly, but
along with the plain people they, too, were thoughtful moon
watchers. No one then or later dared to number the Reverend
Jared Eliot among the hoi polloi, yet he did not hesitate to
advise that the best time to cut brush was "in the months of
June, July, and August, when the old moon that day is in the sign
of the heart." Farmers sowed and harvested crops, pruned fruit
trees, slaughtered hogs, cut firewood, or built fences according
to phases of the moon. Moon watching was serious business for
all. A satellite that could affect the rise and fall of the seas must
have equal if less obvious effect on the rest of nature. Many
settlers brought almanacs with them to America, and New England began to issue its own a decade after settlement. Everyone was familiar with the signs of the zodiac, the shifting of
planets about the sky, the changing positions of constellations.
It is probably an exaggeration, however, to say they were informed or addicted students of astrology. They were attentive
to general predictions laid out in the almanacs, but for guidance
on specific matters they kept an eye on the moon.

A sampling of the lore handed down through the century
reveals that pole beans should be planted when the horns of the
moon are up, to encourage them to climb; but a farmer must
not roof a building then, for the shingles will warp upward. He
should plant root crops during the "dark of the moon" but not
pick apples, which will rot regardless how they are stored. Further admonitions held that

during a new moon a farmer should sow herbs, garlic, radishes,
and hay his meadows but beware that a setting goose will
produce blind goslings,

during a waxing moon he should sow grain but not slaughter
hogs, for they will swell in the barrel,

during a full moon a slaughtered cow will give juicy meat and a
weaned calf will become a good milker,

during a waning moon the farmer should cut timber, split
firewood, and gather fruit and artichokes, but horses born in
this phase will remain weak through life and a slaughtered pig
or sheep will produce only dry meat.

No one in the seventeenth century questioned the validity of
moon farming, and faith in it persisted far into the future. John
Stilgoe cites a comment from the *Farmer's Almanac* of 1979.
"For many generations up to and through the scientific age, the
farmer believed that if the moon can control the tides of the
oceans it can influence the action of the soil," the editor writes.
Science today rejects this supposed wisdom of the past, but
perhaps it is not "altogether unrealistic" to denigrate the much-
scorned moon farming at a time when "skepticism is growing
against the omnipotence of science and its failure to explain
many mysteries of life."

Witchcraft in Salem

No other event has done more to darken the reputation of
seventeenth-century America than the Salem witchcraft trials
of 1692. What follows was published in 1900 by Edward Eggleston, an excellent writer and historian now nearly forgotten.
Literature on the trials was already "oppressively vast" and has
become more oppressively vast since, but Eggleston's eloquent
rendering of the tragic episode stands up well nearly a century
later. It deserves to be revived if only to remind the present of
his marvelous book *The Transit of Civilization,* from which
these pages come.

Salem village, an outlying suburb two or three miles from Salem proper, was almost a frontier town in 1692. Men still wore buckskin breeches and hats with a brim narrow in front and long behind. Wolves, bears, and catamounts were trapped. Some of the settlers had participated in the desperate battle at the Narragansetts' town sixteen years before. The sword and the rapier were still worn at the side, the fowling piece six and seven feet in length was in use. Men had been killed by the Indians in the bounds of Salem within three years. Education was generally neglected; even men of substance were sometimes unable to write. The old patriarchs who had made the settlement had just died off; the community had lost its steadfast guides. New clergymen had come in and new magistrates, not with the education of England, but with the scantier training of New England—a training in which the felling axe was more important than the Latin grammar. The new clergy, men of the second and third generations, were, with a few exceptions, profoundly impressed with the necessity of believing anything ghostly or horrible; the supernatural was the basis of their piety. Increase Mather, the bishop by brevet of New England, had published books on the ominous eclipses of 1680 and 1682, and another in 1686 on Illustrious Providences, which was a storehouse of those dragons' teeth that bore such ample fruit in 1692. His abler but less judicious son, Cotton, had issued a book on "Memorable Providences relating to witchcraft and Possessions." It had come to a second edition in the very year before the horrors of Salem.

The village of Salem had the elements needed for a witchcraft mania—a quarrel between minister and people; a circle of young girls from eleven to twenty, including some who worked as helps, who met at the minister's house and practiced together folk-sorcery and that kind of divining that has been the amusement of such for ages. These girls soon began to manifest symptoms of hysteria and hypnotism; one or two married women also had "fits" in sympathy with them. A doctor called to attend them decided that they were afflicted by "an evil hand." There was some heartless and heedless imposture, no doubt, in what followed, but there was also much of self-deception.

The glimpses of the infernal world that we get in Salem are highly incredible. The witches say prayers by a tall black man with a high-crowned hat—always with a high-crowned hat. They ride on sticks and poles, sometimes they are on brooms, and sometimes three are on one pole. One relates that a pole carrying two broke, but by holding fast to the one in front of her, the witch got safe to her destination. The witches fondle yellow birds, suckling them between their fingers, and one day a girl cries out in meeting that a yellow bird sits on the minister's hat as it hangs on a pin on the pulpit. The witch usually sits on the great crossbeam of the meetinghouse, fondling the yellow bird. One man was seen to nurse two black pigs at his breasts. Sometimes a hog, sometimes a black dog, appears and says, "Serve me." Then the dog or pig "looks like a man," and this man has a yellow bird. Cats naturally abound, white cats and red cats and cats without color. Once a man struck with a rapier at a place designated by one of the girls, and she declared the cat dead and the floor to be all covered with blood. But no one else saw it. This is probably hypnotism, hardly imposture. A great mass of such inconsequent and paltry foolery was believed, not alone by owl-blasted children, but by Stoughton and the other judges, and by pious Samuel Sewall himself, more's the pity! Where is the motive? What prompted the most eminent Christians and leading citizens to prefer so base a life—companions to cats and dogs and devils? Why did the torture of innocent children, this mischief-working witchcraft with endless perdition at the tail of it, give pleasure to rational creatures? The court never once thought to ask.

The trial scenes were perdition. The "afflicted children" screamed, went into spasms, shouted, charged the prisoners with torturing them, and their apparent torments were frightful. They laid to the charge of the accused unheard-of deviltries, such as the killing of wives long dead, attempting to choke aged grandparents, and what not besides. Husbands in some instances turned against wives, in others they adhered to them, were accused themselves, and died with them.

The trials were accompanied by great cruelties. Officers of the law were allowed to plunder the estates of the accused of all movable property. The prisoners had to pay their jail expenses, and many families were utterly impoverished. Prisoners were cast into the dungeon and were "fettered." Goodman Hutchinson complained of certain prisoners for tormenting his wife; additional fetters were put on them, after which Mrs. Hutchinson was "tolerable well." Some were tortured to make them confess; lads were laid neck and heels until the blood gushed from their noses. These were accredited practices at the time. Several died in prison.

The very skill of the accused was against them. One very neat woman walked miles over dirty roads without showing any mud. "I scorn to be drabbled," she said, and she was hanged for her cleanliness. George Burroughs, the minister, was a strong man, much addicted to gymnastics. He carried barrels of cider by inserting his fingers into the bunghole, and held a seven-foot gun at arm's length. He was the devil's man, away with him to the gallows! The first people in the colony became involved. Twenty in all were executed, four or five at a time. Their bodies were ignominiously thrust into holes at the place where they were executed and were scantly covered.

There were brave men and women among them. Giles Corey, an eccentric old man, had at first signed an affidavit of uncertainty about his wife, a woman of piety, and, strange to say, an entire unbeliever in witchcraft. Two of his sons-in-law turned against her, two were for her. But when old Giles was accused he stiffened his neck. He would save his property, which was considerable and might be compromised; he would will it all to his two faithful sons-in-law. He would prove his steadfastness. He made a will, perfect in every part, giving his property to the sons-in-law, and then totally refused to plead and was slowly pressed to death. The constancy of the old man did much to overthrow the partisans of witchcraft. Joseph Putnam, a young man of twenty-two, declared his detestation of the doctrine. He kept some one of his horses bridled and saddled for six months. He armed all his family, and it was understood that he must be taken, if taken at all, pistol in hand. When the mania was at its height he refused to have his child baptized in the village, but carried it to Salem.

The excitement had risen with every arrest. More than fifty badgered souls had confessed that they were witches. Some had fled the country. But the wide extent of the accusations produced a change in the minds of the people. They knew not who would be struck at next. The governor, at length, refused to call the special court together, and after a tedious confinement a hundred and fifty were released by proclamation. The population of Salem had decreased, its business had suffered, and perhaps it never recovered its prosperity. Slowly the people got over the delusion and came to realize the incalculable and irretrievable harm that had been wrought. Judge Sewall, at a general fast, handed up to the minister to be read a humble confession, and stood while it was read. He annually kept a private diary of humiliation. Honor to his memory! The twelve jurymen also signed an affecting paper asking to be forgiven. Cotton Mather, who had been very conspicuous and had published a book about it, never acknowledged himself wrong in this or any other matter. From the time it became unpopular he speaks of the witchcraft trials in a far-away manner, as if they were wholly the work of some one else. He was never forgiven, and probably never ought to have been.

The revulsion was complete. No witches were tried or hanged or "swimmed" in America after the Salem trials. In half a lifetime more the ardor of the English people visibly abated, and few witches were thereafter arrested in England.

Addendum

Eggleston ends his balanced account of the Salem trials with a minor inaccuracy. He errs in saying that with Salem, witchcraft trials ended in America. Virginia held one in 1706, North Carolina in 1712, and doubtless others occurred elsewhere. No accused witch was ever again put to death, but belief in witchcraft continued to flourish. Witches fluttered through the backcountry well into the eighteenth century. They impregnated children with strange diseases, shot hair balls into cattle, put spells upon guns, even changed men into horses, but more benign ways of exorcising their evil spirits prevailed. "The picture of the supposed witch was drawn on a stump or board and shot at with a bullet containing a little bit of silver," goes one account. "This silver bullet transferred a painful and sometimes mortal spell on that part of the witch corresponding with the part of the portrait struck by the bullet."

Other errors—admittedly those of omission and acceptable in a brief report—flaw Eggleston's summary. To depict Salem as a backwater village burdened with factionalism and a high rate of illiteracy helps to explain why the outburst occurred when and where it did but fails to make clear that all early America and Europe, too, accepted witchcraft as a fact of everyday life. England's great jurist Lord Coke defined a witch succinctly—"a person who hath conference with the devil, to consult with him and/or to do his bidding"—and all America nodded in agreement. Massachusetts' Body of Liberties, promulgated in 1641, listed it as a capital crime and drew on the Bible for justification: Exod. 22:18, Lev. 20:27, Deut. 18:10. The explosion at Salem was unique, but it burst from coals that had been smoldering throughout the seventeenth century.

In the sentence "The court never once thought to ask," Eggleston perpetuates a belief that still survives, that the accused at Salem never had fair trials. What is and is not a fair trial differs in time and with those who make the judgment. By modern standards the Salem trials were unfair. But they were trials, each with judges and juries composed of the accused's peers. Every participant, accused included, accepted as fact that witches were servants of the Devil who could destroy men, beasts, and even communities if they went unpunished. Given this background, recent scholars tend to agree with an opinion handed down by Chadwick Hansen: the Salem trials and trials of witches elsewhere in early America offer "a genuinely exemplary record," especially when compared to Europe's treatment of witchcraft. A few facts. In 1665 Ralph and Mary Hall, who lived in a village on Long Island, were indicted "upon suspicion of witchcraft." The trial was held in New York, possibly to keep local prejudices at a distance. The court concluded that after "having well weighed the evidence, we find there are some suspicions by the evidence of what the woman is charged with but nothing considerable of value to take away her life. But in reference to the man we find nothing considerable to charge him with." The wife was freed in the custody of her husband and thereafter both disappear from history.

In Salem fifty people confessed to being witches, twenty died, thirty were acquitted. Elsewhere in Massachusetts hundreds more were accused during the hysteria; none died. Throughout seventeenth-century America, Salem excepted, sixteen witches were executed. Meanwhile, in Europe, a bloodbath prevailed. In France during the same century nine hundred witches died in a single city and another five thousand in a single province. "It can be added," Peter Shaw writes, "that by some estimates five hundred thousand people were burned as witches between the fifteenth and seventeenth centuries in Europe, most of them being first subjected to dreadful tortures." Most historians ignore this record. This leads Shaw to wonder why they have failed "to ask how New Englanders managed to avoid the enormities committed during the European and English witchcraft crazes," but have instead "linked this country's witchcraft record to a putative tradition of intolerance throughout American history." Scholars in the main accept Arthur Miller's judgment in *The Crucible* that the Salem episode exemplifies an ugly, repressive side of the American character, a persistent determination to stifle dissent. Even Chadwick Hansen ends his balanced account with the homily that "the spirit of the witch hunt is still with us." A virtue of Eggleston's brief account is that it treats the Salem affair for what it was—a unique aberration. Also, it might be added, it was one of those events which, in James Deetz's words, gives the present "a sense of culture shock as profound as if we had encountered a member of any other of the world's exotic cultures." Finally, by calling into question convictions about the invisible world that the settlers had long held, it helps to carry them into an equally strange world—the eighteenth century.

13

The Countryside—North

I N OCTOBER 1704, Sarah Kemble Knight, aged thirty-eight, set out alone on horseback on a trip from Boston to New York. She picked up companionship along the way, often with the post rider, for New England had a mail service now. She endured shabby inns where village topers often kept her awake at night; meals that varied from the unpalatable to almost decent; rocky, unmarked ways that sometimes led into dead ends; but not once did anyone attempt to rob her or threaten her with bodily harm. It did not disconcert her to wake up one night and find she was sharing the room with two men in a nearby bed. The few times she thought her heart might stop came while crossing a stream in a tippy dugout canoe or on a ride to the next stage during a moonless night "that rendered every object formidable," when "every lifeless trunk with its shatter'd limbs appear'd an armed enemy, and every little stump a ravenous devourer."

As a person born and bred in Boston, she saw sights alien to her way of life. Indians lolled about in every village, all destitute but feared by no one. They "trade most for rum, for which they'd hazard their very lives; and the English fit them generally as well by seasoning it plentifully with water." Blacks were not uncommon in Boston—about 3 to 4 percent of the population—but she disliked them and it displeased her to find the people of Connecticut "too indulgent (especially the farmers) to their slaves, suffering too great familiarity from them, permitting them to sit at table and eat with them (as they say, to save time) and into the dish goes the black hoof as freely as the white hand." Social distinctions were few in the country. She saw no opulent houses. Old-fashioned titles like "goodwife" and "goodman" had dropped from use. The people were "generally very plain in their dress," although some women followed the fashions, "that you may know where they belong."

Country people and the way they expressed themselves fascinated Madam Knight. One day she had for companions a farmer on an old mare with his daughter mounted behind. The mare was a hard trotter and the girl had only a thin pad for a pillion.

"Lawful heart, father!" the girl shouted between bounces, "this bare mare hurts me dingeely, I'm direful so, I vow."

"Poor child," said the father, "she us't to serve your mother so."

"I don't care how mother us't to do," said the girl in a passionate tone ("at which," Madam Knight reported, "the old man laughed and kicked his jade o' the side, which made her jolt ten times harder").

Garrulity was not a pronounced characteristic among those Knight met. At one stop a man wearing mocassins and ragged dress came in, sat down, began to pull on his pipe, and for a quarter of an hour said nothing. Finally, the host asked, "How do's Sarah do?"

"As well as can be expected," came the answer, and that ended the matter.

A longer exchange recorded by Madam Knight reveals how country people conducted business. The scene that follows occurred in a general store in New Haven.

> In comes a tall country fellow, with his cheeks full of tobacco, for they seldom lose their cud but keep chewing and spitting as long as their eyes are open. He advanced to the middle of the room, makes an awkward nod, and spitting a large deal of aromatic tincture, he gave a scrape with his shovel-like shoe, leaving a small shovel full of dirt on the floor, made a full stop, hugging his own pretty body with his hands under his arms, stood staring round him, like a cat let out of a basket. At last, like the creature Balaam rode on, he opened his mouth and said:
> "Have you any ribbon for hatbands to sell, I pray?"

At this point, if usual procedure followed, the owner asked, "What do you pay in?" Country people were accustomed to four forms of transaction: "pay," which involved an exchange of provisions such as grain, pork, or beef at rates set by the central government but seldom acknowledged by merchants; "pay as money," that is, in Spanish pieces of eight, rials, or shillings minted in Massachusetts Bay; pay in "hard money," silver coins minted in England; or "trust," credit on terms buyer and seller could agree on. A sixpenny knife would cost in "pay" twelve pence worth of provisions; "pay as money," eight pence; in "hard money," six pence; in "trust," whatever was agreed upon.

"The questions and answers about the pay being past," Madam Knight goes on, "the ribbon is brought out and opened."

> Bumpkin simpers, cries "it's confounded gay, I vow," and beckoning to the door, in comes Joan Tawdry, dropping about fifty curtesies and stands by him. He shows her the ribbon.
> "Law, you," says she, "it's gent [genteel]. Do you, take it, 'tis dreadfully pretty."
> Then she inquires, "Have you any good silk, I pray?" which being

brought and bought, "Have you any thread silk to sew it with?" says
she, which being accommodated with they departed.

They generally stand after they come in a great while speechless,
and don't say a word till they are asked what they want, which
I impute to the awe they stand in of the merchants, who they
are constantly almost indebted to, and must take what they
bring without liberty to choose for themselves; but they serve
themselves well, making the merchants stay long enough for their
pay.

Madam Knight took care not to dismiss bumpkin and his
spouse as fools, "for these people have as large a portion of
motherwit, and sometimes larger, than those who have been
brought up in cities, but for want of improvements render
themselves almost ridiculous, as above."

If, after the visit to New York, Madam Knight had continued
into New Jersey and Pennsylvania she would have found different countrysides populated by people with even stranger ways
and manners, but still country people akin to those in New
England. Farmers of the Middle Colonies, like those Madam
Knight had observed, kept a tight hold on the past—the wonders of the invisible world continued to influence their lives—
but in spite of themselves had already been pulled toward the
eighteenth century. They lived in a fairly stable world of isolated farms with only occasional excursions beyond them. A
rare few could be called poor. Their health was good. ("In this
respect it is worth noting a recent finding," Jim Potter has
written, "that has indicated that human stature in America
reached a peak around the end of the colonial period and then
remained more or less constant until the middle of the twentieth century.") The language they spoke was becoming American, an amalgam of accretions, dialects, and accents from a
variety of sources. Social distinctions were minimal and would
remain so through the coming century. Little of this held true
for the countryside in the South.

The Countryside—South

A Frenchman who visited Virginia toward the end of the eighteenth century said, "It is in this state, for the first time since I crossed the sea, that I have seen poor people." Scattered in among the opulent plantations "one often finds miserable huts inhabited by whites, whose wan looks and ragged garments bespeak poverty." The rich had aggrandized the best land everywhere, and "these whites, without means and often too without ambition, are thus restrained on all sides and are reduced to the small number of acres they have been able to acquire." The wide gap between rich and poor in the Chesapeake that the Frenchman saw in 1782 had already appeared before the seventeenth century ended.

By 1700 the farms of those who had prospered in the Chesapeake had become plantations, none the palatial Tara of Scarlett O'Hara's day, but all nonetheless substantial affairs. One plantation owner, William Fitzhugh of Virginia, described his way of life in 1686. He owned 23,500 acres of unsettled land, all fronting on water, which he expected someday to sell at a large profit. His plantation consisted of another thousand acres, seven hundred of these still forested but the remainder "good, hearty, plantable land without any waste either by marshes or great swamps." A mile and a half upstream lay his gristmill, "whose toll I find sufficient to find my own family with wheat and Indian corn for our necessities and occasions." He also owned twenty-nine slaves, "a choice crew of Negroes, . . . most of them this country born," and among them "a considerable parcel of breeders [who] will keep the stock good forever."

His house was "furnished with all accommodations for a comfortable and genteel living." It had a large cellar, brick chimneys, and thirteen rooms, nine of them "plentifully furnished." "Plentifully" was the right word, to judge by an order sent a few years later to his agent in London wherein he asked to have sent over "two large silver dishes containing about eighty or ninety ounces each dish . . . a dozen of silver plates . . . two silver bread plates . . . a pair of silver candlesticks large and fair . . . a pair of silver snuffers and stand." The outbuildings consisted of slave quarters plus "a dairy, dovecote, stable, barn, henhouse, kitchen, and all other conveniences, and all in a manner new." An orchard of "about twenty-five hundred apple trees, most grafted," was "well fenced with a locust fence, which is as durable as most brick walls." The kitchen garden, also well fenced, measured a hundred square feet. A "good stock of cattle, hogs, horses, mares, sheep, etc.," rounded out the holdings.

In the midst of this opulence lay the miniscule holdings of ordinary farmers. Their everyday lives did not differ radically from those of northern farmers. "They always had plenty of plain food and raiment, wholesome and good, suitable to their humble station and the times in which they lived," Devereux Jarratt, the son of a plain family, recalled in old age. "Our food was altogether the produce of the farm, or plantation, except a little sugar, which was rarely used; and our raiment was altogether my mother's manufacture, except our hats and shoes, the latter of which we never put on but in the winter season. We made no use of tea or coffee for breakfast, nor at any other time; nor did I know a single family that made any use of them. Meat, bread, and milk were the ordinary food of all my acquaintance."

Chesapeake farmers differed from their northern counterparts in several ways. First, approximately a third had lost title to their lands and become tenants of plantation owners, a trend that would increase during the oncoming century. Second, religion played a smaller part in their lives, or so it would appear from the recollections of Jarratt, who later became a priest in the Anglican church.

There was a church in the parish within three miles of me, and a great many people attended it every Sunday. But I went not once in a year. And if I had gone ever so often, I should not have been much the wiser, for the parish minister was but a poor preacher— very unapt to teach or even to gain the attention of the audience. Being very nearsighted and preaching wholly by a written copy, he kept his eyes continually fixed on the paper, and so near that what he said seemed rather addressed to the cushion than to the congregation.

Third, plain farmers in the South were clearly aware of their lower social status. As quoted earlier, when a poor Virginia farm boy saw a man on a horse trotting down the road

with a wig on, it would so alarm my fears and give me such a disagreeable feeling, that, I dare say, I would run off as for my life. Such ideas of the difference between *gentle* and *simple* were, I believe, universal among all of my rank and age.

Despite their obviously inferior status even the lowest among the poor whites had those they could look down upon—the enslaved blacks. By the end of the century slaves had all but replaced indentured servants as a labor force. Blacks comprised 11 percent of the population in Maryland, 28 percent in Virginia, and 43 percent in South Carolina, percentages that would increase throughout the eighteenth century.

Town Life

Everyday life in the countryside differed sharply from that in the port towns, which also differed sharply from town to town. Boston, though stagnating at the end of the century and soon to be eclipsed by Philadelphia, was cultured, affluent, and seemed "more like an old English town than any in America." Solemn Quakers set a sedate tone for young Philadelphia. New York was the liveliest place on the continent. Its narrow streets were lined with neat brick houses faced with colored tiles, and the Dutch housewives wore earrings. A visitor soon learned that the Battery "was a good way for a stranger to fit himself with a courtesan, for that place was the general rendezvous of the fair sex of that profession after sunset . . . [and] there was a good choice of pretty lasses among them, both Dutch and English." It was a heavy-drinking town. Even at public auctions "they treat with good liquor liberally, and the customers drink liberally and generally pay for't as well by paying for that which they bid up briskly." "To drink stoutly," said another visitor, "is the readiest way for a stranger to recommend himself." Also, he added, "to talk bawdy and to have a knack at punning passes among some there for good sterling wit."

A diversity of people set town life apart from the countryside. In the country, ethnic groups lived unto themselves. In Philadelphia a man could sit down to a dinner in a tavern "with a very mixed company of different nations . . . Scots, English, Dutch, and Irish." In New York, travelers could hear French and Hebrew in the streets and Dutch spoken as much as English, even among blacks. A man from the Chesapeake looking for the road into town recorded a conversation between his slave and a black girl who mixed Dutch with her Pidgin English.

> "Dis de way to York?" says Dromo.
> "Yaw, dat is Yarkiee," said the wench, pointing to the steeples.
> "What devil you say?" replied Dromo.
> "Yaw, mynheer," said the wench.
> "Damme you, what you say?"
> "Yaw, yaw."
> "You damn black bitch."

By the end of the century problems that rarely concerned the countryside infected townspeople's daily affairs. In the early years of settlement their lives differed little from those led in an English village. Most families had a milk cow that grazed on the commons, a pig or two that roamed through the neighborhood, a kitchen garden that fed them through much of the year. As American villages became towns, patterns changed. Where did one dispose of the garbage? Firewood, once close by, had to be hauled in from a distance and became expensive. Fire became an omnipresent fear; one in Boston in 1679 destroyed some 150 buildings. Disease spread rapidly; an epidemic of smallpox came to be expected every decade or so in the crowded towns. Care for the indigent became a problem. As the poor increased, so too did the crime rate. Without a police force how did a town control crime, let alone bawdy houses and unlicensed, raucous grogshops? All these and other urban problems appeared in the port towns before 1700; much of the oncoming century would be spent seeking ways to solve them.

Still, given the drawbacks, few townsmen would have traded places with their country cousins. The townsman did not necessarily eat better, but his menu could vary more if he lucked upon a wife who could and liked to cook. All the port towns had public markets—Philadelphia's met twice a week, on Wednesdays and Saturdays—that displayed the pride of the countryside. Strangers were constantly surprised by the new dishes placed before them. One visitor from the Chesapeake who came to New York reported, strange to say, that there "I dined upon what I never had eat in my life before, a dish of fried clams." Later he remarked that "they have a diversion here, very common, which is the barbecuing of a turtle to which sport the chief gentry in town commonly go once or twice a week." In Boston he came upon another delicacy new to him—"salt codfish, which here is a common Saturday's dinner, being elegantly dressed with sauce of butter and eggs."

A townsman also had a more varied social life than the countryman, who could break routine only with an occasional husking bee, house-raising, or the weekly visit to church. The townsman had neighbors all around, and within a few minutes walk the local public house, be it a tavern, inn, or grogshop. Grogshops dotted the waterfront and offered those who worked in the area cheap drink and the closest thing to dens of iniquity found in early America. Back from the water were modest inns that catered to farmers in town for market day, peddlers, and other small-time tradesmen. The better sort of people patronized taverns, which generally gave excellent meals and drinks, good company, and clean rooms. Men did not drop into a public house simply for a drink; they came for the afternoon or evening or both. Sailors read posted notices for available berths. Bulletin boards told what ships were in port, what ones were sailing and where. Mail was directed to the house an addressee was known to favor. America had no newspapers until the eighteenth century, but English papers and journals were available in the taverns, as were chess and backgammon boards for those who wished to play. For both the better and meaner sort, the public house was a home away from home.

A public house attracted a clientele shaped along class lines. The leatheraprons, or working men, went to their watering spots, shopkeepers to theirs, while certain taverns catered only to gentlemen, easily spotted by their embroidered waistcoats and ruffled shirts, their curled and powdered hair. By 1700 the distance between upper and lower classes in the port towns had widened to the point where gentlemen, who comprised only 10 percent of the population, owned 40 percent of the wealth. Ironically, American settlement began with the colonists relatively equal in wealth, although everyone believed in a hierarchical society. Now the century was ending with a hierarchical society entrenched in the port towns and the South, while to farmers in the northern countryside the facts of everyday life suggested that all men were created equal.

SELECTED BIBLIOGRAPHY

The general rule has been to include mainly books and articles quoted in the text and occasionally material that helps to flesh out the background of a particular topic.

Allen, David Grayson. *In English Ways: The Movement of Societies and the Transferal of English Local Law and Custom to Massachusetts Bay in the Seventeenth Century.* 1981.

——. " 'Vacuum Domicilium': The Social and Cultural Landscape of Seventeenth-Century New England." In *New England Begins.* Vol. 1, pp. 1–52.

Axtell, James. "The Ethnohistory of Early America: A Review Essay." *William and Mary Quarterly,* 35 (1978), pp. 110–44.

——. *The European and the Indian: Essays in Ethnohistory of Colonial North America.* 1981.

Berthoff, Rowland. *An Unsettled People: Social Order and Disorder in American History.* 1971.

Beverley, Robert. *The History and Present State of Virginia.* Edited by Louis B. Wright. 1705. Reprint. 1947.

Boorstin, Daniel. *The Americans: The Colonial Experience.* 1958.

Boyer, Paul, and Stephen Nissenbaum. *Salem Possessed: The Social Origins of Witchcraft.* 1974.

Bradford, William. *Of Plymouth Plantation, 1620–1647.* Edited by Samuel Eliot Morison. 1952.

Braudel, Fernand. *The Structures of Everyday Life: The Limits of the Possible,* vol. 1. 1979.

Breen, T. H. *Puritans and Adventurers: Change and Persistence in Early America.* 1980.

Breen, T. H., and Stephen Innes. *"Myne Owne Ground": Race and Freedom on Virginia's Eastern Shore, 1640–1676.* 1980.

Breen, T. H., James H. Lewis, and Keith Schlesinger, "Motive for Murder: A Servant's Life in Virginia, 1678," *William and Mary Quarterly,* 40 (1983), pp. 106–120.

————. "Creative Adaptations: Peoples and Cultures," In *Colonial British America*, edited by Jack P. Greene and J. R. Pole, pp. 195–232.

Bridenbaugh, Carl. *The Beginnings of the American People*. Vol. 1, *Vexed and Troubled Englishmen, 1596–1642*. 1968.

————. *Cities in the Wilderness: The First Century of Urban Life in America, 1625–1742*. 1955.

————. *Early Americans*. 1981.

Bushman, Richard L. "American High-Style and Vernacular Cultures." In *Colonial British America*, edited by Jack P. Greene and J. R. Pole, pp. 345–83.

————. *From Puritan to Yankee: Character and the Social Order in Connecticut, 1690–1765*. 1967.

Calhoun, Arthur W. *A Social History of the American Family*. 3 vols. 1917–1919.

Carr, Lois Green, and Lorena S. Walsh. "The Planter's Wife: The Experience of White Women in Seventeenth-Century Maryland." *William and Mary Quarterly*, 34 (1977), pp. 542–71.

Chastellux, Marquis de. *Travels in North America in the Years 1780, 1781, and 1782*. Edited by Howard C. Rice. 2 vols. 1963.

Chinard, Gilbert, editor. *A Huguenot Exile in Virginia: Or Voyages of a Frenchman Exiled for His Religion with a Description of Virginia and Maryland*. 1934.

Coolidge, John. "Hingham Builds a Meetinghouse." *New England Quarterly*, 34 (1961), pp. 435–61.

Craven, Wesley Frank. *The Colonies in Transition, 1660–1713*. 1968.

————. *The Southern Colonies in the Seventeenth Century, 1607–1689*. 1949.

————. *White, Red, and Black: The Seventeenth-Century Virginian*. 1971.

Crevècoeur, St. John de, *Sketches of Eighteenth Century America*. Edited by Henri L. Bourdin, Ralph H. Gabriel, and Stanley T. Williams. 1925.

Cronon, William. *Changes in the Land: Indians, Colonists, and the Ecology of New England*. 1983.

Danckaerts, Jasper. *Journal, 1679–1680*. Edited by B. B. James and J. F. Jameson. 1913.

Deetz, James. *In Small Things Forgotten: The Archaeology of Early American Life*. 1977.

Demos, John Putnam. *Entertaining Satan: Witchcraft and the Culture of Early New England*. 1982.

————. *A Little Commonwealth: Family Life in Plymouth Colony.* 1970.

Duffy, John. *Epidemics in Colonial America.* 1953.

Dunn, Richard S. "Servants and Slaves: The Recruitment and Employment of Labor." In *Colonial British America,* edited by Jack P. Greene and J. R. Pole, pp. 157–94.

Earle, Alice Morse. *Home Life in Colonial Days.* 1898. Reprint. 1974.

Earle, Carville V. *The Evolution of a Tidewater Settlement System: All Hallow's Parish, Maryland, 1650–1783.* 1975.

Eggleston, Edward. *The Transit of Civilization from England to America in the Seventeenth Century.* 1900. Reprint. 1959, with an introduction by Arthur M. Schlesinger, Sr.

Ferling, John E. *A Wilderness of Miseries: War and Warriors in Early America.* 1980.

Fitzhugh, William. *William Fitzhugh and His Chesapeake World, 1676–1701: The Fitzhugh Letters and Other Documents.* Edited by Richard Beale Davis. 1963.

Fletcher, Stevenson Whitcomb. *Pennsylvania Agriculture and Country Life, 1640–1840.* 1971.

Furnas, J. C. *The Americans: A Social History of the United States, 1587–1914.* 1969.

Galenson, David W. *White Servitude in Colonial America: An Economic Analysis.* 1981.

Galenson, David W., with a rebuttal by Mildred Campbell. " 'Middling People' or 'Common Sort'? The Social Origins of Some Early Americans Reexamined." *William and Mary Quarterly,* 35 (1978), pp. 499–540.

Gallman, James M. "Determinants of Age at Marriage in Colonial Perquimans County, North Carolina." *William and Mary Quarterly,* 39 (1982), pp. 176–191.

Glassie, Henry. *Pattern in the Material Folk Culture of the Eastern United States.* 1968.

Greene, Jack P., and J. R. Pole, eds. *Colonial British America: Essays in the New History of the Early Modern Era.* 1984.

Greven, Philip J., Jr. "Family Structure in Seventeenth-Century Andover, Massachusetts," *William and Mary Quarterly,* 23 (1966), pp. 235–256.

Hall, David D. "Literacy, Religion, and the Plain Style." In *New England Begins.* Vol. 2, pp. 102–58.

Hamilton, Dr. Alexander. *Gentleman's Progress: The Itinerarium of*

Dr. Alexander Hamilton, 1744. Edited by Carl Bridenbaugh. 1948.

Hammond, John. *Leah and Rachel.* 1656. Reprinted in *Tracts and Other Papers, 1836–1846,* ed. Peter Force. Vol. 3, no. 14.

Handlin, Oscar. "The Significance of the Seventeenth Century." In *Seventeenth-Century America,* edited by James M. Smith, pp. 3–12.

Hansen, Chadwick. *Witchcraft at Salem.* 1970.

Hartley, Dorothy. *Lost Country Life.* 1979.

Haskins, George Lee. *Law and Authority in Early Massachusetts: A Study in Tradition and Design.* 1960.

Hawke, David. *The Colonial Experience.* 1966.

Hellier, Thomas. Memoir edited by T. H. Breen, James H. Lewis, and Keith Schlesinger. "Motive for Murder: A Servant's Life in Virginia, 1678." *William and Mary Quarterly,* 40 (1983), pp. 106–20.

Hemphill, C. Dallett. "Women in Court: Sex-Role Differentiation in Salem, Massachusetts, 1636–1683," *William and Mary Quarterly,* 39 (1982), pp. 164–75.

Henretta, James A. "Families and Farms: *Mentalité* of Pre-Industrial America." *William and Mary Quarterly,* 35 (1978), pp. 3–32.

————. "Economic Development and Social Structure in Colonial Boston." *William and Mary Quarterly,* 22 (1965), pp. 75–92.

————. "Wealth and Social Structure." In *Colonial British America,* edited by Jack P. Greene and J. R. Pole, pp. 262–89.

Hindle, Brooke, ed. *America's Wooden Age: Aspects of Its Early Technology.* 1975.

————, ed. *Material Culture of the Wooden Age.* 1981.

Holmes, Oliver Wendell. Essay on John Winthrop, Jr., as physician, reprinted in Samuel Eliot Morison, *Builders of the Bay Colony,* pp. 284–88. 1930.

Hooker, Richard J. *Food and Drink in America: A History.* 1981.

Hosmer, Uncle Ben. Quoted in "Culture and Cultivation: Agriculture and Society in Thoreau's Concord," by Robert A. Gross. *Journal of American History,* 69 (1982), pp. 42–55.

Howell, Charles, and Allan Keller. *The Mill at Philipsburg Manor, Upper Mills and a Brief History of Milling.* 1977.

Hume, Ivor Noël. *Martin's Hundred.* 1982.

Isaac, Rhys. *The Transformation of Virginia, 1740–1790.* 1982.

Jarratt, Devereux. "The Autobiography of Devereux Jarratt, 1732–1763." Edited by Douglass Adair. *William and Mary Quarterly,* 9 (1952), pp. 360–68.

Jennings, Francis. *The Invasion of America: Indians, Colonialism, and the Cant of Conquest.* 1975.

Josselyn, John. *An Account of Two Voyages to New-England.* 1674.

Kammen, Michael. *People of Paradox: An Inquiry Concerning the Origins of American Civilization.* 1972.

Knight, Sarah Kemble. *Journal.* 1825. Reprinted in *The Puritans: A Source Book of Their Writings,* edited by Perry Miller and Thomas H. Johnson. 2 vols. 1963.

Kupperman, Karen Ordahl. "Apathy and Death in Early Jamestown," *Journal of American History,* 66 (1979), pp. 24–40.

Langdon, George D., Jr. *Pilgrim Colony, 1620–1691.* 1966.

Laslett, Peter. *The World We Have Lost.* 1965.

Leach, Douglas Edward. *Arms for Empire: A Military History of the British Colonies in North America, 1607–1763.* 1973.

Lemon, James T. "Spatial Order: Households in Local Communities and Regions." In *Colonial British America,* edited by Jack P. Greene and J. R. Pole, pp. 86–122.

McMahon, Sarah F. "A Comfortable Subsistence: The Changing Composition of Diet in Rural New England, 1620–1840," *William and Mary Quarterly,* 42 (1985), pp. 26–65.

McManis, Douglas R. *Colonial New England: A Historical Geography.* 1975.

McNealy, Terry A. "Bristol: The Origins of a Pennsylvania Market Town," *Pennsylvania Magazine of History and Biography,* 95 (1971), pp. 484–510.

Main, Gloria. *Tobacco Colony: Life in Early Maryland, 1650–1719.* 1982.

Merwick, Donna. "Dutch Townsmen and Land Use: A Spatial Perspective on Seventeenth-Century Albany, New York," *William and Mary Quarterly,* 37 (1980), pp. 53–78.

Miller, John C. *The First Frontier: Life in Colonial America.* 1966.

Morgan, Edmund S. *American Slavery—American Freedom: The Ordeal of Colonial Virginia.* 1975.

———. *The Puritan Dilemma: The Story of John Winthrop.* 1958.

———. *The Puritan Family: Religion and Domestic Relations in Seventeenth-Century New England.* 1944. Reprint. 1966.

Nash, Gary B. *Red, White, and Black: The People of Early America.* 1974.

———. "Social Development." In *Colonial British America,* edited by Jack P. Greene and J. R. Pole, pp. 233–61.

————. *The Urban Crucible: Social Change, Political Consciousness, and the Origins of the American Revolution.* 1979.

New England Begins: The Seventeenth Century. 3 vols. 1982.

————. 3 vols. 1982. A catalogue to an exhibition presented by the Museum of Fine Arts, Boston, produced under the direction of Jonathan L. Fairbanks and Robert F. Trent.

Notestein, Wallace. *The English People on the Eve of Colonization, 1603–1630.* 1954.

Pearce, Roy Harvey. *The Savages of America.* 1953.

Potter, Jim. "Demographic Development and Family Structure." In *Colonial British America,* edited by Jack P. Greene and J. R. Pole, pp. 123–56.

Powell, Sumner Chilton. *Puritan Village: The Formation of a New England Town.* 1963.

Roeber, A. G. "Authority, Law, and Custom: The Rituals of Court Day in Tidewater Virginia, 1720–1750," *William and Mary Quarterly,* 37 (1980), pp. 29–52.

Rothman, Daniel J. "A Note on the Study of the Colonial Family," *William and Mary Quarterly,* 23 (1966), pp. 627–34.

Russell, Howard S. *A Long Deep Furrow: Three Centuries of Farming in New England.* 1976.

Rutman, Darrett B. and Anita H. *A Place in Time: Middlesex County, Virginia, 1650–1750.* 1984.

————. *Winthrop's Boston.* 1965.

————, and Anita H. Rutman. "Of Agues and Fevers: Malaria in the Early Chesapeake," *William and Mary Quarterly,* 33 (1976), pp. 31–60.

St. George, Robert Blair. " 'Set Thine House in Order': The Domestication of the Yeomanry in Seventeenth-Century New England." In *New England Begins.* Vol. 2, pp. 159–351.

Shaw, Peter. Review of *Entertaining Satan,* by John P. Demos. *New Criterion,* December 1982, pp. 81–84.

Shea, William L. *The Virginia Militia in the Seventeenth Century.* 1983.

Sheehan, Bernard W. "Indian–White Relations in Early America: A Review Essay," *William and Mary Quarterly,* 26 (1960), pp. 267–86.

————. *Savagism and Civility: Indians and Englishmen in Colonial Virginia.* 1980.

Sheridan, Richard B. "The Domestic Economy." In *Colonial British America,* edited by Jack P. Greene and J. R. Pole, pp. 43–85.

Shryock, Richard H. "British versus German Traditions in Colonial Agriculture," *Mississippi Valley Historical Review,* 26 (1939), pp. 39–54.

Shy, John. "A New Look at Colonial Militia." *William and Mary Quarterly,* 20 (1963), pp. 175–85.

———. *Toward Lexington: The Role of the British Army in the Coming of the American Revolution.* 1965.

Smith, Daniel Blake. "The Study of the Family in Early America: Trends, Problems, and Prospects." *William and Mary Quarterly,* 39 (1982), pp. 3–28.

Smith, James M., ed. *Seventeenth-Century America.* 1959.

Smith, John. *The General History of Virginia, New England, and the Summer Isles.* 1624. Edited by Edward Arber in 1889, printed in two volumes in 1910 with a long introduction by A. G. Bradley.

Smith, Timothy L. "Congregation, State, and Denomination: The Forming of the American Religious Structure." *William and Mary Quarterly,* 25 (1968), pp. 155–76.

Stilgoe, John R. *Common Landscape of America, 1580 to 1845.* 1982.

Tate, Thad W., and David L. Ammerman, eds., *The Chesapeake in the Seventeenth Century: Essays on Anglo-American Society.* 1979.

Trent, Robert F. "Arms and Armor." In *New England Begins.* Vol. 1, pp. 53–65.

———. "Coastal Algonkin Culture, 1500–1680." In *New England Begins.* Vol. 1, pp. 66–93.

———. "New England Joinery and Turning before 1700." In *New England Begins.* Vol. 3, pp. 501–50.

Vaughan, Alden T. "Blacks in Virginia: A Note on the First Decade." *William and Mary Quarterly,* 29 (1972), pp. 469–78.

———. " 'Expulsion of the Salvages': English Policy and the Virginia Massacre of 1622." *William and Mary Quarterly,* 35 (1978), pp. 57–84.

Waters, John J. "Family Inheritance, and Migration in Colonial New England: The Evidence from Guilford, Connecticut," *William and Mary Quaterly,* 39 (1982), pp. 64–86.

Winslow, Ola Elizabeth. *Meetinghouse Hill, 1630–1783.* 1952.

Wood, Peter H. *Black Majority: Negroes in Colonial South Carolina from 1670 through the Stono Rebellion.* 1974.

Zuckerman, Michael. "The Fabrication of Identity in Early America," *William and Mary Quarterly,* 34 (1977), pp. 183–214.